REAGANOMICS
VS.
THE
MODERN
ECONOMY

REAGANOMICS

VS.

THE

MODERN ECONOMY

THE
CONFLICT
THAT DIVIDES AMERICA

MICHAEL DOUGLAS GILBERT

NORTH LOOP BOOKS,
MINNEAPOLIS

NORTHLOOP
BOOKS

North Loop Books
322 First Avenue N, 5th floor
Minneapolis, MN 55401
612.455.2294
www.NorthLoopBooks.com

ISBN-13: 978-1-63413-981-6
LCCN: 2016913839

Distributed by Itasca Books

Cover Design by Emily Keenan
Typeset by Mary Kristin Ross

Printed in the United States of America

For Carolyn Sue Gilbert
and Deborah Gilbert

Contents

Introduction

Ronald Reagan inspired optimism from the moment he gave his first inaugural address on January 20, 1981. Reagan famously declared that "government is not the solution; government is the problem." With the enemy identified, the plan of attack was obvious. Reagan advocated less government, lower taxes, and fewer business regulations as the remedy for America's problems. This policy, later dubbed Reaganomics, was widely heralded as a call to action against the federal government in Washington.

Reaganomics has dominated public policy discussions in the United States since 1981, largely because of Ronald Reagan's personal popularity and the huge improvements in the economy during his administration. When Reagan, a Republican, took office after Democratic president Jimmy Carter, the American economy was wallowing in inflation, low output, and high unemployment—a phenomenon called "stagflation." By the end of Reagan's eight years in office, the economy had improved dramatically. Inflation and unemployment were lower and output was higher. There was, however, one rather ominous sign: the national debt had nearly tripled.

By the time he left office, Reagan's policies had apparently saved the country. The handsome former movie star and California governor became the most influential figure in America since Franklin D. Roosevelt. Indeed, Reaganomics seemed calculated to undermine FDR's New Deal, Lyndon Johnson's Great Society, and all the "big government" programs that had been associated with Democrats since the 1930s.

But the improvements in the American economy in the 1980s had nothing to do with Reaganomics. High oil prices stemming from the OPEC cartel's oil embargoes had caused the stagflation that inflicted so much damage to the US economy. In time, a dramatic increase in non-OPEC oil production would break the cartel's hold on petroleum prices. Market forces, not Reaganomics, worked beautifully to end stagflation. But the market correction would take nearly ten years. That was plenty of time for confusion and Reagan's personal popularity to overwhelm any rational assessment of Reaganomics.

Confusion would also mask the real cause of the savings and loan crisis in the 1980s, as well as the leveraged buyouts, greenmail, and insider trading on Wall Street that led to turmoil in the corporate world. Tax cuts and increased defense spending during the Reagan administration brought the biggest peacetime budget deficits in US history. Once the world's biggest creditor nation, the United States became the world's largest debtor nation. For all its political appeal, Reaganomics seemed to do actual harm.

In order to make a proper assessment of Reaganomics, we need to understand our modern economy: the complex, interconnected system of jobs, markets, and government services that we rely on for our very survival. We seek some defining quality of a modern economy, some timeless characteristic that separates it from the economic world inhabited by our primitive ancestors. Technology is an important feature of our economy, but it changes every day. The defining characteristic we seek is the impossibility of true self-sufficiency. We are dependent on the system around us, and that system includes government.

Unlike Americans in the eighteenth-century world of the founding fathers, people in a modern economy have no recourse to go out into the wilderness, build a log cabin, and supply themselves with food, clothing, and other necessities of life. For practical purposes, nobody produces any necessities for themselves; if possible, they buy them from a store, typically with money they earn from a job. But this presents an immediate problem: people can't get to their job, or to the marketplace, without infrastructure. Moreover, people must have enough education to function in a modern economy, even if they can't afford a private school. Their security requires more than just a gun to protect their home; national defense and police protection are important. The solution to these and many other problems makes government an important part of the economy.

This does not bode well for the economic theory known as Reaganomics. Any arbitrary attack on government threatens to undermine the system that everyone—old and young, rich and poor, conservative and liberal—depends on for their very survival. Yet opposition to government seems to come naturally to Americans. We will explore this opposition further in chapter 4.

We will also explore frustrations and divisions within the Republican Party, which can be traced to the party's loss of power in the Great Depression. The GOP was the dominant force in national politics until FDR came along. Beginning in the 1930s, the Democrats offered policies that most Americans found appealing, policies closer to the requirements of a modern economy than anything Republicans had to offer. The Republicans had to wait until 1980 for Ronald Reagan to revive the Grand Old Party.

The misconception that somehow Reagan turned the economy around in the 1980s has so distorted domestic policy that for many Americans, it is axiomatic that the path to prosperity and increased freedom is to attack, shrink, shut down, ridicule, and underfund government. But the proper economic function of government in a modern economy is to provide necessities like public infrastructure and national defense, necessities that cannot be adequately obtained from the private sector market-place. The need for these necessities doesn't go away just because confusion and Ronald Reagan's continuing popularity can be leveraged to get votes.

This book systematically presents the definition and characteristics of our modern economy, and the impact of public policies on our everyday lives. We are concerned with needs; i.e., goods and services that people cannot do without. Needs cost money, whether they are obtained while shopping in the marketplace or by paying taxes for public services. So we are interested in where money goes, whether for personal consumption, savings and investment, or taxation.

Recent economic history reveals the conflicts between the demands of a modern economy and the dictates of the economic theory known as Reaganomics. Though Reagan's most prominent critic, Republican George H. W. Bush (president from 1989–1993), straightened out some of the problems with Reaganomics, there was still enough faith in the theory to produce a second spate of Reaganomics in the George W. Bush administration (2001–2009). The results were all too predictable.

In this book, we learn how political frustrations and denial of economic reality led to the Great Recession, a huge national debt, partisan bickering, a dysfunctional Congress, and political statements that often border on sedition. None of this would have happened without the confusion that surrounded Reaganomics. Ironically, from all indications, Ronald Reagan would have been offended by the exploitation of his personal popularity to undermine the routine functions of the American government that are so essential to our modern economy.

We want to understand how the decades-long attack

on government has created an economic system that works extremely well for the few but doesn't adequately meet the needs of the many. Chapters 1 and 2 define the characteristics of a modern economy and provide context for all that follows. The history (chapters 3–5) that led to Reagan's election precedes an in-depth discussion of Reaganomics, first as an economic policy (chapters 6–9), and then as a political strategy (chapters 10–12). The history of Reaganomics provides empirical evidence that the proper structure of public policy in a modern economy is precisely the opposite of Reagan's policies.

In part IV, we combine what we know about the requirements of the modern economy with our experiences with Reaganomics. This allows us to construct public policy that produces optimum levels of employment, consumption, and investment. Put simply, our goal in this book is to define the proper relationship between markets and government in a modern economy.

We'll begin by taking a look at the features that distinguish our modern economy from the primitive economies that preceded it.

Part I

The Modern Economy and Resistance to Government

Chapter 1
The Modern Economy

Across the political spectrum, Americans sense that neither their economy nor their government is working properly. But these two problems aren't unrelated. In ways that we often take for granted, our economic system determines many of the proper functions of government. Before reacting emotionally, Americans need to understand the nature of the modern economy—the complex, interconnected system that they rely on for their very survival.

The modern economy is defined by characteristics that are part of our everyday experience. We expect to buy the necessities of life and perhaps a few luxuries from the marketplace. Buying requires money, which we typically obtain from some form of employment. But neither our employer nor sellers in the marketplace will build a road from their front door to our front door: that task lies with the government. If we relied on markets alone, buyers and sellers couldn't easily interact with each other; neither could employers and workers.

Markets alone are therefore inadequate to support the markets. We cannot rely solely on the private sector for such basic needs as roads, physical security, and adequate education. Also, left to their own devices, markets allow and even encourage activities that we find offensive: environmental pollution, dangerous working conditions, and product misrepresentations. Meanwhile, many hardworking people earn so little that they cannot afford all the necessities of life.

We correct these problems by pooling our resources through government and paying for public goods and services, including regulation, with some form of taxation. General opposition to government, however, often makes it impossible to correct market problems. Crumbling public infrastructure, unafford-able college tuition, the 1980s savings and loan (S&L) crisis, the Great Recession, budget deficits, a huge national debt, and even a dysfunctional Congress can all be attributed to resistance to the public sector's proper role in the economy. These items will be discussed in much more detail later in the book. For now, we know that opposition to government, often based on simplistic notions like "let the market handle it," provides no guidance to solving problems that exist precisely because the market doesn't "handle it."

The Primitive Economy

Our early ancestors provided for themselves by hunting and gathering the necessities of life. In their primitive world, the list of necessities was short: food, clothing, shelter, and with any luck, a degree of security. But over many centuries, people have greatly improved their lives with new inventions, greater knowledge of the world, labor specialization, advances in health care, and increased efficiency.

A *primitive economy* is one in which it is possible for a person or a small group of people to provide themselves with all the necessities of life. They are not dependent on others for their needs. A *modern economy* is one in which virtually no one provides themselves with any of the necessities of life. People must have money to buy necessities from a complex, interconnected system of producers, distributors, and sellers. In this system, govern-ment has to fill the gaps if the private sector does not adequately provide certain necessities. People's survival requires that the system around them works properly.

Today, people work in specialized jobs and almost never

produce any necessities for themselves. Farmers and ranchers, for example, produce food but they too are dependent on the fruits of the modern economy: electricity, tractors, fuel, and medical care for both themselves and their animals. Everyone is part of an interconnected economic system that must work in order for them to work—and survive.

The transition from a primitive economy to a modern economy was the most significant change in the history of economics, and occurred unevenly across the world. Even within the same country, some areas could develop more rapidly than others. Brazil, for example, has huge modern cities like São Paulo and Rio de Janeiro; yet there are indigenous tribes in the Amazon basin that have primitive economies. More typically, tribal people avail themselves of the benefits of their country's modern economy. Residents in the far north of Canada, for example, can hunt with rifles and navigate with GPS. When necessary, they are transported by airplane to get advanced medical care. These indigenous people are no longer truly self-sufficient.

Independence in a primitive economy allowed an actual economic disassociation from other people. But in a modern, interdependent economic system, economic "independence" equates with either a good job for most people or high net worth for a few. In any case the system must work to protect everyone's interests.

We may say that an economy remains primitive as long as living independently of others is both possible and actually done by a significant number of people.

The Economy of the Founding Fathers
The late eighteenth-century economy of America's founding fathers had some characteristics that were similar to our own. People earned money working in trades, retailing, and the profes-

sions. Some of them lived in towns and cities. But they could go west, build log cabins, grow crops, hunt for food, provide their own security, and live independently of the rest of the country. The early United States still met the minimum requirements of a primitive economy. An unhappy clerk in Boston or Philadelphia would have been wise not to complain about a bad boss or commuting to work. It was better than fighting off Indians, bears, and rattlesnakes in an insect-infested wilderness.

The founding fathers were unfamiliar with many of our problems. They could ride a horse across pastures and between trees, so there was little need for public infrastructure, outside of cities at least. Medicine was so primitive that home remedies might be preferred to a doctor. Benjamin Rush, a prominent physician and friend of both John Adams and Thomas Jefferson, still practiced blood-letting.[1] Educational standards were minimal and illiteracy was common. People often worked on farms or learned a trade as an apprentice to a skilled craftsman.

Early Americans certainly appreciated the importance of national defense, the post office, and the judicial system. But many of our present-day concerns are unique to our complex, modern economy and its reliance on government. George Washington, for example, had little, if any, worries about environmental pollution, let alone climate change. Benjamin Franklin had no reason to believe that inadequate financial regulation might bring down the whole economy. High unemployment was of little concern if one could simply create a life for oneself in the Western wilderness. Government played only a small part in the eighteenth-century economy: people had so little money that an extensive tax system was impossible. It is easy to see why the founding fathers have little or nothing to offer us as guidance in the relationship between government and our modern economy.

The Frontier Spirit—an Impediment to Good Policy?

As long as people could move to wilderness areas and build a life for themselves independent of others, the United States still met the minimum requirements of a primitive economy. Well into the nineteenth century, Americans had the option to settle sparsely inhabited areas. The settlement of the West produced a widespread "frontier spirit" in the United States that permeated all aspects of American life. Americans saw themselves as rugged individualists who provided for their own needs, took risks, and created new businesses. Those who thrived in "primitive" conditions were tough and resourceful.

This uniquely American sense of independence still drives entrepreneurial activity, creates new products, and accounts for much of the nation's prosperity. It is a good thing, of course; except when it is not. In America's modern economy, everyone must rely on the system around them to work properly in order to make money to support themselves and their families. The mismatch between economic reality and the lingering myth of frontier independence makes many Americans susceptible to public policies incompatible with economic reality. They easily succumb to appeals to their sense of freedom to oppose government-provided necessities—necessities that cannot come from anywhere else.

Europe had extensive settlements a millennium before the United States became a nation. With no frontier to escape to, Europeans tackled market inadequacies more readily than Americans. The controversy between "European socialism" and "American free markets" highlights the trade-off between modern economic reality (which includes a role for government) and giving full reign to a market economy that will often disappoint us.

Even today, wealthy Americans retreat on the weekend

to farms and ranches to live a simulated frontier life complete with television and air-conditioning. They hunt, fish, raise farm animals, and grow a few crops. The nearby rural grocery store doesn't match up to urban supermarkets, so they see themselves as roughing it in the wilderness. They can maintain the myth of independence in a primitive economy, disassociated from their fellow citizens and unfettered by government (except for the state highways, without which they couldn't get to their weekend cottage). America's lingering frontier spirit seems innocuous but may stand in the way of realistic public policy.

Market Inadequacies and Market Defects

We may define *markets* as the prevailing private sector system that provides us with goods and services. We owe most of our material well-being to the success of our market-based economy. Because markets are flexible, always adjusting to surrounding circumstances to approach an equilibrium of supply and demand, we can truly say that markets always "work"! This is the case even if businesses succeed or fail, unemployment is at 25 percent, or babies are dying of starvation or lack of medical care. Markets always work toward an equilibrium of supply and demand.

Our concern with these potentially brutal market results stems from the fact that we live in a modern economy. We are part of a system that must work in order for us to supply ourselves with the necessities of life. So the inadequacies of the market economy are of great interest to us. We recognize three broad types of market inadequacies:

- **Markets may be *irrelevant* to our needs.** There are no acceptable private sector solutions to national defense, public infrastructure, or police protection. Profit-seeking insurance companies will gladly administer Medicare

Advantage plans as government contractors to the Medicare system, but they will not insure senior citizens in any other way. We rely on government to satisfy these critical needs.

- **Markets may have *internal defects* that offend us.** The profit incentive that drives most market activity may cause businesses to cut costs or take shortcuts. These businesses may not adequately dispose of toxic waste or provide employees with safety equipment. Businesses may attempt to profit from defective or misrepresented products. So Americans work through their elected officials in the executive and legislative branches of government to protect themselves from the consequences of these predictable internal market defects.

- **Markets always work, of course, but the results may be *insufficient*.** This means that the routine operations of the market economy may not adequately accommodate the needs of willing and able workers who seek to support themselves in the only way possible in a modern economy—by working in a job that will allow them to buy the necessities of life. Remember that unlike their primitive ancestors, people in a modern economy do not have the option to forcibly wrest necessities from the world around them by dint of their own labor.

Market insufficiencies often arise from problems in the labor markets such as unemployment or inadequate employment. *Inadequate employment* is defined to be a job with some defect that, over the course of a lifetime working in the job, will prevent a person from providing himself with all the necessities of life.

The four defects that cause inadequate employment are

insufficient compensation (hourly wages or weekly salary), too little work (too few hours, seasonal work, or an unstable industry), lack of benefits (e.g., a pension, savings plan, or medical insurance), and difficult working conditions that could shorten a person's career or even his life. Note that labor markets determine whether or not these defects exist.

Many American families can only overcome widespread inadequate employment by having more than one wage earner. Market forces are the main cause of what some people consider to be the disintegration of the traditional family model of a working husband and a stay-at-home wife and mother. The dramatic increase of women in the workforce over the last half century can be attributed to economic necessity as much as women's understandable desire for greater job satisfaction.

The four defects that give rise to inadequate employment are not the only threats to people who try to work and support themselves. Later we will discover more subtle, but very real, market forces that can minimize employment opportunities in a modern economy.

The Role of Nonprofit Organizations

Our definition of markets as the prevailing private sector system that provides goods and services includes both nonprofit and for-profit organizations. Businesses eager to make a profit will try to satisfy demand for goods and services. But "demand" requires that a prospective purchaser must be both willing and able to buy. Sometimes critical needs like food, clothing, and shelter are unmet due to market insufficiency. Nonprofit organizations such as charities and churches play a valuable role in assisting needy people.

These organizations are widely accepted by their communities. People recognize that they fulfill critical needs. The existence of such nonprofit organizations is proof that profit-seeking private sector markets alone are inadequate to meet all our needs.

However, in a huge, modern economy, even massive assistance from nonprofit organizations may not be enough to make up for the deficiencies of the private profit-seeking markets. In the wake of the 2007–2009 Great Recession, community food banks and church food pantries faced unprecedented demand. But so many people were hungry that the nation also had forty-eight million people collecting food stamps (the government's Supplemental Nutrition Assistance Program). For this and many other reasons, government is a critical part of a modern economy.

The Five Categories of Government Economic Functions

In a representative democracy like the United States, people can use government to overcome structural problems in the private sector marketplace. Indeed, the proper economic function of government is to provide necessities that are not adequately available from the markets. This naturally gives rise to five categories of government economic functions, each named for the specific market inadequacy that makes it necessary:

- Category I   Total Market Irrelevancy
  These are needs provided by government for which there is no market solution for anyone. National defense, public safety, disaster relief, homeland security, the criminal and civil justice systems, monetary policy, public infrastructure, public health, the Coast Guard, and Medicare are obvious examples. So is the use of fiscal policy to stimulate an economy in a steep economic downturn. Assistance for the severely mentally ill often requires resources like police and a special court system that are outside the usual private sector health-care system.
- Category II   Internal Market Defects
  Government regulates certain market behaviors that

unfortunate past experiences tell us will cause harm. Regulations address our concerns about product safety (especially in food, medicines, and transportation), unsafe working conditions, environmental pollution, and misrepresentations of financial products. Minimum-wage legislation is critically important to workers who might otherwise be subjected to life-threatening levels of compensation determined solely by supply and demand in the labor markets. Unfortunately, federally mandated minimum wages have never been sufficient to prevent inadequate employment.

- Category III Predominant Market Insufficiency
These are necessary services provided by government that most people are unable to provide for themselves. Examples include Social Security, universal public education (grades K–12), and financing higher education and vocational training. To be sure, many people have pensions or savings for retirement. Some people can afford to send their children to private schools. But in general, inadequate employment and occasional unemployment make it impossible for most of the population to pay directly for their children's education or to reliably save enough for retirement. Providing medical services and disability payments for injured veterans is also a Category III function, along with social services that protect the elderly and people with serious mental or physical problems.

- Category IV Acute Market Insufficiency
This describes government services that satisfy needs that are so acute as to be potentially life-threatening. Category IV functions provide some people help with

problems that most of the population are capable of solving for themselves. Examples include food stamps, unemployment compensation, welfare, Medicaid, insurance subsidies through the Affordable Care Act, public housing, and protective services for children. People who need Category IV services may have problems that are not caused by markets; but these are proper functions of government because markets offer inadequate solutions.

- Category V   General Market Insufficiency

These are important government services that supplement available private sector offerings that the public deems to be inadequate. One example is basic research. This is defined to be long-term investigations in technical fields that are not likely to pay off anytime soon. Past experience has shown that such government-funded research in medicine, technology, and energy can provide big future economic benefits to the nation. Certain NASA programs fall into this category (others may be valuable for national defense, which would make them Category I government functions).

National Public Broadcasting is another example of a Category V government function. There are huge numbers of commercial radio and television channels, but the American people still see value in providing media outlets not controlled by commercial interests. Public recreation areas, America's system of national parks, and the US Postal Service are also Category V functions.

Everyone recognizes the need for at least some government services from each of the five categories. Yet most discussions of economics treat government as if it were an unwelcome guest at a party reserved for markets alone. In the next chapter, we'll explore this natural antigovernment bias, along with widespread misunderstanding about both public services and the taxes that pay for them.

Chapter 2
The Public Sector Imperative

If possible, we prefer to let the private sector take care of our needs if it can do so adequately. There are several reasons for this. A private sector solution eliminates the contentious public controversies about how government will provide a service and how to pay for it. Private firms have a profit incentive to be productive (in fairness, public employees can also be offered incentives in the form of bonuses). Finally, the markets have a long history of innovation that often yields surprising benefits.

But the five categories of government services described in the last chapter arise naturally because of inadequacies in the private sector. So why do we assume, against overwhelming evidence to the contrary, that markets alone are sufficient to meet all our needs? Perhaps it's because economics is widely viewed as the study of a free market economy. This neat theory would only be tainted by complications like unemployment, poverty, natural disasters, sickness, altruism, charity, redistribution, bad luck, and the need for public services, which we will discuss next.

Government: The Ultimate Service Provider
Government almost always provides services, versus tangible goods. Typically, tangible public goods such as public infrastructure or defense equipment are made by private sector firms under contract to the government.

So government spending either flows through private sector contractors or is paid to government employees. The former make profits; the latter become consumers. Businesses routinely sell products to government contractors and to military personnel, public school teachers, astronauts, police officers, and national park rangers. Government is not some alien phenomenon; it is an important part of the modern economy.

There may be disagreements over the exact categorization of various government economic functions. The important thing is to recognize the critical role of government in a modern economy. We have mainly listed federal government services; but market inadequacies are so pervasive that state, county, and local government services are just as necessary. For example, the US Department of Agriculture enforces federal laws governing food handling and processing. At the local level, food inspectors often barge uninvited into restaurants and other businesses that sell food in order to enforce regulations on behalf of the public. The people's decisions to regulate food handling and other business activities are beneficial almost all the time.

Our pervasive use of government goods and services is simply a practical solution to market inadequacies. In the twenty-first century, people who graduated from public schools drive their private vehicles on public streets to private sector jobs. These same individuals pay taxes to support police officers who might shop at their employer's business. This mix of public and private sector activity is not some injection of socialism into a capitalist system; it is simply the way a modern economy works.

When Can the Market Handle It?
Since there is often some apparent overlap between private sector and public sector economic activity, it may not always be clear when government should have a role in economic activity. For example, retirees can sign up for either traditional Medicare or Medicare Advantage plans. The private sector provides numerous products to the military. There are both public and private golf

courses. Private charter schools offer education to public school students. Given the multitude of options, can we develop criteria that help us decide whether or not we must rely on government for some of the necessities of life?

Let's look at some services that seem to fall in the gray area between the private sector and the government. Perhaps they can offer us some guidance.

- **Halliburton in Iraq:** In the second Iraq War (the one that began in 2003), Halliburton, the Houston-based oil field services provider, acted as a defense contractor to provide both food services and truck drivers. To the extent that dining halls were located outside of active combat areas, food services were no different than any other contracted public or private sector service designed to satisfy a temporary need. But sending unarmed, untrained civilian truck drivers into combat zones was something else entirely. These jobs are clearly military functions. An overzealous attempt to show that markets could handle everything unnecessarily risked civilian lives. Some contractors were killed while providing these services.

- **Security Contractors:** A government contractor was hired to protect high-profile visitors to Iraq during the second Iraq War. This increased the costs to taxpayers for what had historically been a military function. The contractor was not part of any military chain of command, a potentially serious issue in an occupied country. Moreover, these security jobs were highly prized assignments for regular military personnel since they were much less dangerous than actual combat operations. It was bad for morale to give the most plum jobs to highly paid mercenaries. A war zone isn't the best place to experiment with swapping expensive "market solutions" for Category I government functions.

- **Privatizing Social Security:** When the stock market is doing well, some people invariably call for replacing Social Security with private savings accounts. Social Security, a Category III function of government, has often been called the most successful government program. It helps satisfy a critical retirement need for most Americans. Private sector retirement accounts that replaced Social Security would be subject not only to market risks but also to well-known problems in the financial sector such as high fees, bad advice, and self-serving financial advisors. By the time someone retires, it may be too late in life to overcome these market problems. Lesson: Some government functions are just too important to turn over to the private sector.

- **The Center for Disease Control and Prevention:** Private sector pharmaceutical companies routinely develop drugs to combat numerous diseases. Medical providers treat illnesses. So why do we need a government agency to deal with threats like Ebola and the Zika virus? These deadly illnesses often arise suddenly and then evolve to thwart treatment and prevention efforts. They can spread rapidly. So the CDC's activities are more akin to national defense than to market activity. These Category I government functions are necessary because markets are ineffective at solving these existential problems. Again, some problems are just too important to risk the possibility that well-known inadequacies in the private sector will leave them unsolved.

- **Medicare Advantage Programs:** Medicare Advantage programs were injected into the Medicare system in 2003. They were a new version of the old Medicare Choice plans and were designed to promote the illusion that there was a private sector substitute for an inherently public sector activity. To enhance that illusion, Medicare Advantage programs were required to offer extra benefits that were not available from traditional Medicare (hence the word "advantage"). Recall that Category I functions like Medicare exist precisely because there is no market solution. So it is not surprising that this artificial use of private sector insurance companies to administer Medicare has caused problems. Medicare Advantage plans have greatly reduced choices of health-care providers while subjecting senior citizens to private sector companies with a financial incentive to deny them coverage.

Lessons: Even if we nominally prefer private sector solutions, it is risky to try to thwart economic reality. If markets are the solution to a problem, it should not be necessary for government to artificially create a profit incentive to attract them. Even more important, some needs are just too critical to be at the mercy of clumsy market processes.

Federal Spending: Paying the Bills

When the federal government spends money (and it must), bills come due and are usually paid from tax revenue. Taxation is thus a consequence, not a cause, of federal spending. This may be counterintuitive. In the private sector, spending is ultimately determined by income. By contrast, the need for federal government income (i.e., tax revenue) is determined by spending. Since the American government responds to societal needs (!) and not simply to the availability of money, it is not possible to reduce federal government spending by cutting taxes. This was illustrated in 2001 when a big cut in federal income taxes was followed by years of increased government spending.

Cutting taxes in 2001 did not stop terrorist attacks, wars, natural disasters, baby boomer retirement, or a big downturn in the economy due to inadequate financial sector regulations. We will discuss these things later in the book, but for now we can just observe that taxes are at worst a neutral concept. Taxation is good because it pays the nation's bills. But taxes will always be a contentious issue because no one wants to pay them.

For the first two hundred years of the nation's history, people in both parties agreed that it was important to rein in any excessive national debt. This conservative view was motivated by two important concerns: If we let debt get out of hand and then something untoward happened (e.g., a war or terrorist attack), then the debt could spiral upward with compound interest. Also, each generation should pay its own bills. Future generations would have their own problems and should not be burdened by past generations' as well. In recent years, the United States has abandoned these conservative principles largely because public figures can use promises of tax cuts to get elected to office. It is easy for them to take advantage of antigovernment sentiment.

Natural Antigovernment Bias
It often seems like we come out of the womb griping about government. Why are many people readily amenable to any arguments opposing taxation, regulations, or government programs?

We can better understand *natural antigovernment bias* by comparing our experiences in the markets with our interactions with government. In the marketplace, we buy an ice cream cone or a new shirt, get a haircut or go to a spa, take a vacation or get our car repaired. But with government, we get summoned to jury duty, serve in the military and get shot at, pay taxes, stand in line to renew our driver's license, or pay to get our car inspected. Why are there such huge differences between these two types of experiences? We noted earlier that the American people pool their resources through government in order to provide themselves with necessities that markets fail to provide. Government is often the collection of all the annoying things that the private sector cannot profit from. We inflict these government experiences on ourselves out of necessity.

Since the second half of the twentieth century, antigovernment bias has become the default value for a public overwhelmed by wars, assassinations, oil embargos, public corruption, complex technology, globalization, terrorist attacks, economic downturns, and partisan bickering. After more than two hundred years, Americans' view of their government can still be characterized as one of distrust and confusion. Yet their economy—the modern economy—cannot function properly without government. This contradiction is a structural problem that has often interfered with good public policy. Politicians have always found it easy to exploit confusion about the proper relationship between the public and private sectors. Throughout American history, the tail of politics has often wagged the dog of economic reality.

$E = M + G$

As noted before, in our modern capitalist economy, markets cannot work without public infrastructure, public safety, public education, and many other public services. Opposition to government is therefore also opposition to markets. Clearly, a successful modern economy requires both markets and government services.

Our economic system fails when, through no fault of their own, people cannot obtain the necessities of life. The Great Depression and the Great Recession come to mind. But markets always work toward an equilibrium of supply and demand. So how is it possible that the economy can fail? A simple equation will provide some clarification. Our economic system (E) includes both markets (M) and government (G).

Symbolically, and significantly, $E = M + G$.

So E fails if there is not enough G to compensate for market inadequacies.

Alternatively, $G = E - M$ reminds us that the public sector is the part of the economy that markets fail to handle adequately.

Markets determine the need for government in our economy. We have taxation because it is almost the only way we can pay for public services. In other words, we pay taxes because we have government, and we have government because we have markets. Hence, we have to pay taxes because we have a market economy. In the modern world, to believe in markets is to believe in both government and taxation.

In the next chapter and the rest of part I, we'll learn more about how major events in American history shaped our views of public economic policy.

Chapter 3
The New Deal and the Rise of Democrats

In chapters 1 and 2, we learned why both markets and government are essential parts of our modern economic system. As we discovered, opposition to government may lead to public policies that threaten ordinary people's survival. While there was no particular day on which America completed its transition from a primitive economy to a modern economy, the Great Mississippi River Flood of 1927 is a good place to begin understanding the modern relationship between people, markets, and government.

A Call for Intervention: The 1927 Flood

In 1927, unrelenting rain in the Mississippi River Basin flooded the central United States. The river and all its tributaries overflowed their banks and flooded homes, farms, businesses, and towns. The flood threatened lives and greatly limited commercial activity in the central United States, especially anything that required river transportation.

Republican president Calvin Coolidge selected his secretary of commerce, Herbert Hoover, to lead relief efforts. Hoover was an excellent choice. An orphan who worked his way through Stanford University, Hoover went on to make a fortune as a mining engineer. He then left the business world and followed his Quaker beliefs to devote himself to humanitarian causes. Hoover led relief efforts in Europe during and after World War I, and these experiences plus his organizational skills served him well as he coordinated the joint federal and state response to the flood. This achievement enhanced Hoover's already solid reputation and contributed to his victory in the 1928 presidential election.[2]

The Great Mississippi River Flood was a huge event that had

two important long-term economic implications in American life, one big and dramatic and the other more subtle. For the first time in the nation's history, the federal government acted on a massive scale to assist people for a reason other than national defense. The American people learned that when necessary, they could use their national government to address problems far beyond the capabilities of either state and local governments or private sector markets.

The Great Flood offered another important lesson as well. Americans all across the nation had demanded federal help for flood victims. They sympathized with the hundreds of thousands of people who lacked food, homes, jobs, or even dry land to stand on. But it wasn't just compassion that prompted calls for relief. The Mississippi River and its tributaries together constituted the nation's largest transportation system, and the reduction in barge and riverboat traffic had impeded commerce all across the nation.

Many people west of the flood couldn't get their goods to market. People on dry land east of the flood couldn't receive products, including raw materials they needed for manufacturing. The demands for a large flood-relief effort were motivated as much by commercial concerns as by humanitarian considerations.

We now take for granted that the federal government will respond to large natural disasters. Efforts to save lives and help people get back on their feet after a flood, hurricane, tornado, or forest fire are important Category I government functions. Today the Federal Emergency Management Agency works with state governments and private sector organizations like the American Red Cross to restore some semblance of normalcy to survivors who may have lost their homes, their jobs, and even their loved ones. Yet until 1927, the US government played only a small role in people's lives. Aside from military service in times of war, about the only contact that most people had with the federal government was mail delivery from their friendly neighborhood postman.

By 1927, the United States had a modern economy: an interconnected system of production, distribution, and sales that might at times depend on the public sector for its success. Near-future events would confirm this interdependence.

The Bubble Bursts: October 1929

Many factors together created the huge economic downturn known as the Great Depression. These included excessive debt, natural disasters, inadequate government regulations, unrealistic optimism, and movements of capital between nations.

In the early days of World War I, American farmers had borrowed heavily to expand production in order to feed both the United States and Europe. America entered the war in 1917 and, not coincidentally, the war ended in 1918, much sooner than expected. The US agricultural sector found itself with overproduction, low commodity prices, and heavy debt. Moreover, the 1927 flood devastated farmers in the center of the nation. In 1930, the Dust Bowl brought ruin to many farmers and ranchers in Oklahoma, Texas, Kansas, and other states.

Apart from more serious events like the 1927 flood, the roaring twenties was a period of irrational exuberance. This decade encouraged irresponsible borrowing, especially in the stock market, where it seemed that every clerk, doctor, shoeshine boy, and businessman could make their fortune simply by buying low and selling high. Lack of financial regulation, an important Category II government function, turned Wall Street into the new Wild West.

Insiders on Wall Street could form a syndicate, buy the

slow-selling stock of some obscure company, and then publicly proclaim that this firm was the next big thing. The public would snap up the company's stock and its price would soar accordingly. This self-fulfilling prophecy encouraged more stock purchases. The syndicate would then sell its shares at a handsome profit and move on to repeat this now-illegal "pump and dump" scheme.

Overpriced stocks bought with borrowed money, overexpansion in the industrial and agricultural sectors financed by excessive debt, loss of jobs to mechanization,* lack of financial regulation, excessive capital investment at the expense of consumption, and natural disasters that weakened large portions of the country made the US economy more fragile than anyone realized. It wouldn't take much to burst the bubble.

In October 1929, England raised interest rates to attract capital that had been lured by speculative profits in the United States. The sudden reduction in money for capital investments led to a massive sell-off at the New York Stock Exchange. For most Americans, the October 29, 1929, stock market crash heralded the beginning of the Great Depression.[3]

Lower stock prices and lack of capital caused loan defaults, business bankruptcies, and foreclosures on homes and farms. Unemployment soared, eventually reaching 25 percent. Hunger and misery swept the land. Families merged households in order to survive. Previously, Americans had gone about their lives secure in their beliefs that they were just like their primitive eighteenth- and early nineteenth-century ancestors. They now discov-

---

*   You don't have to be an Einstein to understand the impact of mechanization, but it doesn't hurt. In a 1933 speech in Pasadena, California, the great physicist Albert Einstein said that, especially in America, the Great Depression was mainly caused by technological advances that "decreased the need for human labor," which, in turn, resulted in a decline in consumer purchasing power. See Walter Isaacson, *Einstein: His Life and Universe* (New York: Simon & Schuster, 2007), 403.

ered that they were part of an interconnected modern economy that had to work properly if they were to work—and live—at all. Self-sufficiency wasn't an option.

Republican president Herbert Hoover was unfairly blamed for the economic catastrophe, a reminder of a peculiar fact of American politics: voters often attribute credit or blame for big economic events to the current occupant of the White House, irrespective of actual causes.

No Market Solution

President Hoover responded to the economic downturn by expanding federal government infrastructure construction. This increased employment with private sector government contractors. Hoover also made loans available to states for both infrastructure projects and state-funded economic relief for suffering people. But why all this government spending? Why not just let the market handle it?

Unfortunately, a market economy has no solution to an abnormally steep economic downturn. This is a consequence of the defining characteristic of a free market economy: people make choices based on their own self-interest. In the Great Depression, the unemployed had little or no money to spend. People fortunate enough to keep their jobs feared for the future and reduced consumption. This hurt the economy. Businesspeople responded to lower consumption by reducing inventory, cutting employees' hours, and even laying people off. Lower inventories hurt manufacturers, distributors, and producers of raw materials. This reduced employment further, which in turn led to even lower consumption. Individual choices in the market economy led to an economic implosion.

Herbert Hoover repeatedly assured the public that things

would get better, but that only lowered his credibility. Despite his faith in the markets, Hoover recognized the obvious need for public sector spending (i.e., a government stimulus plan). The federal government was the only thing big enough to jump-start the economy.

Using government for demand creation in an economic downturn is a policy often associated with the great British economist John Maynard Keynes. But Keynes didn't publish his famous economic treatise until 1936, more than three years after Hoover left office.[4] Economic reality drove Hoover to use government to address problems in the Great Depression, the same reality that motivated Keynes's book. Was Republican Herbert Hoover the first Keynesian president or was John Maynard Keynes the first Hooverian economist? The important thing is that today, using fiscal policy to stimulate an economy in a steep downturn is recognized as a critical Category I function of government.

President Herbert Hoover lost the 1932 presidential election to the Democratic candidate, New York governor Franklin Delano Roosevelt. FDR won easily, capturing electoral votes in forty-two out of forty-eight states. Hoover couldn't overcome either the blame for the Great Depression or Roosevelt's perpetually bubbly personality. The scion of a wealthy New York family, Roosevelt chose to devote his life to public service. He had contracted polio in 1921 but never let that misfortune diminish his innate optimism, political ambitions, or concern for the plight of ordinary people. Roosevelt's story was every bit as compelling as that of the orphaned child, Herbert Hoover.

Roosevelt's New Deal

Roosevelt readily accepted the Hoover administration's view that the federal government needed to play a role in ending the Great Depression. Hoover had used government contracts to businesses in an attempt to increase economic activity. As a conservative Republican, he had refrained from any direct federal employment to reduce joblessness. But Roosevelt had the benefit of hindsight. In most people's eyes, Hoover's actions were inadequate. Under FDR, federal programs would be larger and far more aggressive.

The New Deal would begin dramatically in the famous first hundred days of Roosevelt's presidency in 1933 when he proposed much greater federal involvement in the nation's effort to help down-and-out Americans. Eventually, Roosevelt's new government programs would employ citizens in a wide range of public works projects, many of which bypassed the private sector completely. The Public Works Administration and the Civilian Conservation Corps put many thousands of jobless back to work. This was hardly a radical idea. In a modern economy, survival and employment are inseparable for most people.

The fragile financial system was a major problem in the Great Depression. With a nationwide explosion of loan defaults, many people lost money in undercapitalized banks; so Roosevelt declared a bank holiday. Banks were shut down temporarily so that the Treasury Department could examine their books. They were not allowed to open again until their finances were in order. Bank regulation is a Category II government function.

The Social Security Administration, a critical Category III function of government, was created in 1935. Other New Deal initiatives dealt with problems in the agricultural sector. New programs to prevent soil erosion and to increase output were Category V functions of government. The American people accepted this expansion of government because the nation's economic circumstances were so dire. People believed that doing something, even experimentally, was better than doing nothing. There were no private sector alternatives.

The use of government by Hoover and Roosevelt was motivated entirely by practical considerations: huge, life-threatening problems existed in the economy, and the private sector markets were inadequate to solve them. Federal assistance for people in the 1927 Mississippi River flood and federal jobs in the Great Depression weren't offered because of a desire for big government, *per se*, but were necessitated by a conspicuous lack of market solutions.

The Great Flood and the Great Depression showed us that it is both simplistic and impractical to think that markets alone can solve all economic problems.

Emerging Republican Frustrations

During FDR's administration, Democrats came to be seen as the political party whose policies best conformed to the requirements of a modern economy. Republicans were understandably miffed by the rise in Democratic fortunes. The GOP had been the dominant party since the 1860 election of Abraham Lincoln, winning fourteen of the eighteen presidential elections before 1932. But Roosevelt's use of government to help people in times of great economic distress and his personal popularity combined to change America's political landscape for generations.

In the 1930s, Republican complaints about "big government" largely fell on deaf ears. Economic and political reality would ultimately outweigh ideology. For example, some congressional Republicans who opposed Social Security ultimately voted for it; they feared losing their seats in Congress.

But FDR stumbled politically in 1937 when he attempted to "pack" the US Supreme Court in an effort to reduce the influence of older justices who opposed his New Deal programs. This brought intense opposition from members of both parties in Congress. The separation of powers in the federal government is enshrined in the US Constitution. FDR's tactic backfired and effectively ended congressional support for the New Deal. But it was too late for Republicans. The Democrats' use of public sector programs in a time of economic distress had made them more popular than Republicans, and an even bigger need for government was on the way.

Keynesian economics advocates the use of government spending to increase demand in a steep economic downturn, and World War II was its greatest application. Massive deficit spending and direct federal employment to support the government-run war effort obliterated the Great Depression. This set the stage for an expansive postwar recovery that many people consider to be the golden age of American prosperity. Not incidentally, the United States won the war.

The general lesson was clear: government could satisfy big needs that were far beyond the capability of the private sector alone, without jeopardizing long-term prosperity. Debt could be repaid with increased tax revenue from a combination of greater taxable income and higher tax rates on prosperous Americans.

Republican complaints about excessive government rang hollower than ever. The Grand Old Party would try to associate itself with strong national defense, but it was hard to leverage that claim into political advantage, particularly during World War II and the Korean War, when Democrats were in the White House. In later wars, there was enough blame for everybody.

Roosevelt died in 1945 and was succeeded by his vice president, Harry S. Truman, who was elected in his own right in 1948. Republicans wouldn't regain control of the White House until the 1952 election of Dwight D. Eisenhower. There was, however, a new controversy that could potentially attract additional GOP voters—civil rights for black Americans had crept into the national consciousness.

The 1954 *Brown vs. Board of Education* Supreme Court decision stated that "separate but equal" educational facilities were unconstitutional. This promised to rile up enough white voters in the Democratic South to make Republicans a dominant party again. They had lagged behind Democrats in promoting economic recovery during the Great Depression, but now Republicans could use emotional issues like states' rights and forced school integration to attack the federal government.

But Eisenhower wasn't the right Republican to carry an antigovernment banner. One of the greatest military leaders in American history, General Eisenhower was the supreme allied commander in World War II and a lifelong government employee. He enforced court-ordered desegregation in Little Rock, Arkansas, in 1957 and again in New Orleans in 1960. Any thoughts of a Republican advantage from the civil rights movement evaporated.

John F. Kennedy and the Civil Rights Movement

In 1960, Massachusetts Democratic senator John F. Kennedy defeated Eisenhower's vice president, Richard M. Nixon, in one of the closest presidential elections in American history. Kennedy won by only 112,827 votes nationally out of a total of more than sixty-eight million, a 0.17 percent margin. Nixon actually carried more states, twenty-six to twenty-two. But Kennedy won in the electoral college by a 303 to 219 margin, a victory that many Republicans attributed to voter fraud in Illinois and Texas.[5]

Kennedy's father, former Prohibition-era bootlegger and ambassador to Great Britain Joseph Kennedy, had considerable influence in Chicago, where his son's huge margin of victory over-came Nixon's widespread popularity in the rest of the state. In Texas, Kennedy's running mate, senate majority leader Lyndon B. Johnson, had a financially lubricated political machine with a history of alleged campaign violations. Republicans contested the 1960 election, especially in Illinois, but to no avail. Their frustrations hit a boiling point.

President Kennedy initially focused his attention on foreign policy. Events in Cuba had brought the Cold War conflict between the United States and the Soviet Union to America's doorstep. An impoverished third-world country, Cuba had little money and a history of poor leadership. In the 1950s the country was led by Fulgencio Batista, a brutal dictator who suppressed dissent, routinely jailed people for little or no reason, and aligned himself with America's Italian Mafia for personal financial gain. Fidel Castro's 1959 revolution succeeded because even a Communist was thought to be an improvement. The Cubans who had thrived under the dictator Batista fled the dictator Castro and emigrated to South Florida.

Shortly after Kennedy took office in 1961, exiled Cubans from Florida and anti-Communist mercenaries attempted to invade Cuba. Castro reportedly had advanced warning of the Bay of Pigs invasion and it failed miserably. Invaders who weren't killed received long prison sentences. Kennedy had authorized the attack and was roundly criticized for its failure. He would later redeem himself in the 1962 Cuban Missile Crisis, but from the beginning of his administration, Cold War tensions occupied most of Kennedy's time.

In the beginning, civil rights was a secondary concern for the Kennedy administration. After narrowly winning the 1960 election, Kennedy didn't want to take sides in a heated domestic controversy that might jeopardize his chances of winning reelection in 1964. The Republicans had no special advantage on Cold War issues since the overwhelming majority of Americans were solidly and even fanatically anti-Communist. But the GOP hoped to exploit tensions between states and the federal government over court-ordered school desegregation and other inflammatory civil rights issues.

Eventually Kennedy would have to take a stand when blacks across the South bravely stood up for their rights. Civil rights protestors tried to ride Greyhound buses from Washington, DC, to New Orleans but were beaten after stopping in Alabama. Black college students from Tennessee repeatedly risked their lives riding buses into Mississippi, another segregationist bastion. The Kennedy administration actively tried to discourage these Freedom Riders, but for many black Americans and their supporters, there was no turning back. To protect civil rights activists, the president was forced to deploy US marshals and to "federalize" the Alabama National Guard.

Compared with the government's intervention in civil rights, FDR's expanded uses of the federal government in the 1930s and 1940s, first to overcome the Great Depression and then to defeat the Axis powers, were widely accepted by Americans. The former helped people work and support their families; the latter defended the nation. But many people considered support of the civil rights movement to be a far less objective use of federal power. It upset long-standing traditions and threatened to undermine local authority.

While most Americans supported the civil rights movement, the conflict between federal enforcement of constitutional rights and both state and individual opposition to the government's actions would open up a wound of antigovernment resistance that was as old as the nation itself.

Chapter 4
Resistance to Government and the Republican Schism

Antigovernment bias (chapter 2) seems to arise naturally when people fail to recognize that market inadequacies make government the only source of many sometimes-annoying services such as jury duty, tax collection, and automobile registration and inspection. This bias can be corrected with a few moments of introspection. Simply by looking at the economy around them, Americans can see the importance of government.

It is now obvious to everyone in our modern economy that general opposition to government can impede the provision of necessities not adequately available from the private sector. But in the years after the American Revolution, the former colonists were understandably concerned about how their new national government would affect their lives.

Forming the Federal Government

After the Revolution, the United States of America had many important matters to tend to, but under the Articles of Confederation, its first Constitution, the new government had no control over taxation or trade, and no federal executive or judiciary. Article II of this document, which was ratified and enacted on March 1, 1781,* said that each state should retain "its sovereignty, freedom, and independence."[6] This certainly sounded good to former colonists for whom "the United States of America" was largely a foreign concept. But as a practical matter, this created a weak central government and thus, a weak nation.

---

* The Articles of Confederation were agreed to by Congress on November 15, 1777.

National defense was of particular concern. The United States was a small fish in a big ocean dominated by military superpowers like England, France, and Spain, all of whom coveted its land. If attacked, Americans might not have the resources to duplicate their narrow victory in the War for Independence. The nation's leaders understood the need for a more powerful federal government and formed a Constitutional Convention that first met in Philadelphia in 1787. Separately, Alexander Hamilton, James Madison, and John Jay anonymously published *The Federalist Papers*, an influential series of essays that discussed the benefits of a stronger central government. It assured readers that under such a government, their rights would be preserved. The new US Constitution was ratified in 1789.[7]

To eighteenth-century Americans, monarchy was the reference point for oppressive government. So the new Constitution created the familiar system of checks and balances designed to prevent a power grab by some aspiring king. Fortunately George Washington and other early national leaders set high standards for responsible governance, thus erasing fears of any neophyte American royalty. But future generations would be stuck with this sometimes-clumsy system of government. Later, extra-constitutional factors such as political parties, gerrymandering, and Senate filibusters would greatly aggravate the problem. Americans would have to rely on elected officials acting in good faith to make their government work. In time, lack of such good faith would be a much greater threat to the nation than either a monarch or a too-powerful chief executive.

The Whiskey Rebellion

Though the country's new government had few functions by modern standards, it still required some tax revenue to pay its bills. But there were few opportunities for taxation in an economy in which most people had little or no money; so the government looked for commercial transactions in which money or its equivalent changed hands. In western Pennsylvania, whiskey made from surplus corn was used for currency. One-gallon jugs were worth a quarter at local stores. When whiskey distillers were subjected to the Excise Act of 1791, many Pennsylvanians vowed not to pay the hated tax.

Emotions ran high. In Pittsburgh, federal marshals trying to serve writs on delinquent distillers were met with violence. This localized rebellion became a test of the new nation's ability to enforce taxation. Using powers granted by the Constitution, Congress authorized President George Washington to call out state militias to deal with this obstruction to judicial processes. Washington used the militias of four states, including Pennsylvania, to quash the rebellion. Most of the more violent rebel leaders fled but two were arrested, convicted of treason, and later pardoned by the president.[8]

The former colonists had rid themselves of the king and his laws but didn't know what to expect from their new national government. In the eighteenth century, representative democracy under a constitution was as unfamiliar to Americans as airplanes and computers. President Washington's pardon of the ringleaders recognized their forgivable ignorance.

The Federal Land Use Controversy

The new American nation would expand west. Vast amounts of land would be added to the original thirteen colonies by exploration and settlement, taking land from Native Americans, or by treaties with France and Mexico. With the exception of Texas, which had briefly been a separate country and had voluntarily become a state, the thirty-seven states added to the country would be created by the American people through their government. Some of the tens of millions of acres of new land would be sold or given to settlers, railroads, school districts, or speculators. But many millions of acres of undeveloped land would be kept and managed by the federal government. This acreage became a source of controversy as nearby residents sought special land-use privileges at the expense of the land's rightful owners, the American people.

In the twentieth century, and especially during World War II, the sparsely populated West was the beneficiary of huge amounts of federal spending. Even after the war, the federal government maintained military installations in every Western state, which provided tens of thousands of nonagricultural jobs. Defense contractors proliferated in the Western United States.

Thanks to the federal government, every major river in the West was dammed at least once to provide cheap hydroelectric power and water for both human consumption and irrigation. This provided critical support for agriculture and allowed the growth of urban areas. Farms, ranches, cities, and golf courses sprouted in the desert. Per capita government spending was so great in the Western United States that some called it "Uncle Sam's West."[9] But none of the federal largesse helped defuse antigovernment sentiment spawned by conflicts over the use of federal lands. Locals quietly accepted the money and loudly demanded either that they be allowed free use of the land or that the land be given to their states.

Over the years, fanatical and increasingly violent opponents of federal land ownership have often moved back and forth between groups advocating various antigovernment and antisocial doctrines. Some are racist, others anti-Semitic. The so-called

Patriot Movement opposes any exercise of authority by the US government for any purpose other than national defense. Other groups would replace federal authority with "county supremacy." A manifesto of one such group, the Posse Comitatus, threatens to hang government officials at "a populated intersection . . . of streets at high noon."[10] Self-proclaimed "sovereign citizens" are a significant threat to local law enforcement. The police can meet deadly resistance at routine traffic stops. In this environment, opposition to taxation is also a given.

These groups were voting blocs ripe for cultivation by any political organization that would have them. Mainstream office seekers were often too embarrassed to appeal directly to these extremist groups and instead tried to attract them with inflammatory language directed at a wider audience. This strategy worked perhaps a little too well when it also reeled in unsuspecting people who fell for simplistic rhetoric. This created a wedge between otherwise responsible people and most Americans who recognized government's proper place in a modern society.

The Southern Poverty Law Center monitors hate groups across the United States and pursues legal actions on behalf of their victims. The SPLC reported that just after the April 19, 1995, antigovernment terrorist attack on the Murrah Federal Building in Oklahoma City that killed 168 people, 39 percent of Americans agreed with the statement that the federal government is "so large and powerful that it poses an immediate threat to the rights and freedoms of ordinary citizens." By March 2010, 56 percent of Americans shared that opinion.[11] Ordinary citizens forget that they, and they alone, control that "large and powerful" federal government through their elected officials.

States' Rights and Nullification

Local and state interests have often lumped their opposition to laws and regulations emanating from the American government in Washington under the heading "states' rights." But eighteenth-century Americans replaced the Articles of Confederation with the new Federal Constitution precisely because they recognized the need for a stronger national government. Article VI, Section 2, of the Constitution states that, "This Constitution and the laws of the United States, which shall be made in pursuance thereof, . . . shall be the Supreme Law of the land, and the judges in every State shall be bound thereby, anything in the Constitution or laws of any State to the contrary notwithstanding."[12] But that still left many controversies over the federal government's role in resolving regional differences on social issues and civil rights, most of which have economic repercussions.

In 1828, Vice President John C. Calhoun of South Carolina began to promote the doctrine of nullification, the idea that "states can ignore any federal law that goes beyond powers explicitly granted" by the Constitution. Though the doctrine would later be rejected by the courts, Calhoun and other Southerners would use it to defend slavery. It still forms the basis for many attacks on federal authority today.[13]

Under the Constitution, there are at least three states' rights that are inviolable: the right to elect their US senators, their choices for the US House of Representatives, and their votes in the electoral college. The narrow 2000 presidential election between George W. Bush and Albert Gore hinged on Florida's electoral votes. The US Supreme Court took the authority to decide controversies in that election from the state of Florida, and by a five-to-four vote, declared that Bush was the winner. Later, Associate

Justice Sandra Day O'Connor, the swing vote for the conservative majority, said she regretted her vote. O'Connor said that the court only "stirred up the public" and "gave [itself] a less-than-perfect reputation."[14] Perhaps O'Connor recognized the bigger implication of usurping Florida's right to determine its votes in the electoral college: it could be the last nail in the coffin of states' rights.

The mobility of people and the interconnectedness inherent in a modern economy make it possible that anyone in pursuit of work or other economic self-interest could end up just about anywhere in the country. They could be subjected to parochial or even unconstitutional views on social issues. Local interests often hide behind state laws to provide an aura of legality for their peculiar customs. Unfortunately, states' rights have been wielded as a bludgeon to implement and enforce some of the most barbaric laws in America.

States' Wrongs and Segregation

After the Civil War, legalized racial segregation in the South had created a social and economic system that was in some ways worse than slavery. Before Lincoln's Emancipation Proclamation freed the slaves, there was a limit to brutality by slave owners, who had an economic incentive to preserve their valuable property. After Reconstruction, blacks living in the South had no such protection. Blacks were arrested on trumped-up criminal charges or jailed for nonpayment of nonexistent debt ("peonage") in order to provide a steady supply of chain-gang labor. Local governments in the South could earn money contracting this cheap labor to private businesses. Oppression, poor schools, voter discrimination, and racial violence kept blacks from participating in America's economic growth well into the twentieth century.

By the 1960s, blacks in the South had had enough. Mississippi civil rights icon Fannie Lou Hamer told the Credentials Committee of the 1964 Democratic National Convention about the 1963 beating she had received in a Mississippi jail. The beating "left her with severe kidney damage, a blood clot in one eye, and a permanent limp." This type of treatment had been used for generations to keep blacks "in their place" in the South. By the 1960s, blacks had drawn a line in the sand and weren't going to take it anymore. Perhaps Fannie Lou Hamer said it best: "I'm sick and tired of being sick and tired."[15] The most oppressed of Americans had begun their extraordinary quest for freedoms supposedly guaranteed by the Constitution.

Meanwhile, Republicans saw an opportunity to pick up support in the South from white segregationists enraged over the federal government's enforcement of civil rights laws and court decisions. But this would require the GOP to support the states' rights argument for segregation, effectively swapping morality for votes. The future of the Republican Party would be determined by differences within the party over how far it should go in using antigovernment ideology to gain support from fringe groups. This controversy reverberates today.

Three critical factors guaranteed the success of the civil rights movement: the courage of civil rights workers, the brutality of white segregationists, and the new medium of television. Every night in America, people turned on their TV sets to see violent segregationist mobs attacking peaceful protestors. Injustices long hidden by local media were now in plain sight. Legalized racial discrimination would soon disappear as national support for the civil rights movement prompted changes in the law.

There are two important political lessons from the civil rights era, and they are just opposite sides of the same coin. First, foolish and even barbaric laws and policies can be maintained in a state if officials and compliant media hide them from criticism by a larger audience. Second, exposure of issues to a national audience is more likely to produce rational and humane public policy. Gerrymandered congressional districts are an application of the first lesson of the civil rights era, while the use of a president's so-called "bully pulpit" is an application of the second.

Barry Goldwater Unites the Right Wing

During the civil rights era, Democratic president Kennedy and his brother, Attorney General Robert Kennedy, made convenient scapegoats for white segregationists, who couldn't contain their anger as their "way of life" disappeared. Though the Kennedys gave much higher priority to foreign policy and national defense, they were forced to take sides when it became necessary for the federal government to protect civil rights workers in the South. Kennedy's successor, Lyndon Johnson, would push even more aggressively for civil rights.

A sea of hostility emerged against segregationists from a national majority disgusted that there were still vestiges of slavery in twentieth-century America. Southern politicians couldn't very well attribute their losses to heroic black protestors, violent white thugs, or exposure of the truth by television and other media; so "the Kennedys" became the enemy of Southern segregationists. The South would begin to shift its allegiance from the national Democratic Party to the GOP.

Republican Richard Nixon had barely lost to Kennedy in 1960, so the GOP could see that adding vast numbers of former Democrats in the South to the Republican base could spell victory for their next presidential candidate. But this was awkward for the many Republicans who supported civil rights. Could anyone unite a political party divided by such an emotional issue?

Arizona Republican senator Barry M. Goldwater's 1964

presidential campaign put together an informal coalition of interest groups united by one thing: opposition to the federal government. Goldwater added disenchanted Southerners to antigovernment free market purists, opponents of federal land ownership in the West, antitax zealots, and businessmen opposed to federal regulation of commerce. Unfortunately, right-wing hate groups would also become natural allies of the Goldwater movement. This would not sit well with traditional Republican conservatives already disturbed by the inclusion of white segregationists in their party.

Barry Goldwater had voted against the 1964 Civil Rights Bill as a US senator—he thought that legal remedies to racial segregation should be enacted at the state level. But what if the state itself was the problem? How do you clean your hands if you're washing them with dirty water?

The addition of Southern segregationists would magnify a rift in the GOP that had previously been formed by east-west regional differences in the country. Metaphorically, Western Republicans stepped out of their ranch houses and didn't see another soul for miles in any direction. They couldn't understand why anyone needed government for anything other than national defense and local law enforcement. For these Western conservatives like Barry Goldwater, election to public office was an opportunity to attack and shrink government. But Eastern Republicans stepped out of their houses and apartments, saw thousands of people around them, and understood that government was essential in an interconnected modern economy. Republicans like New York governor Nelson Rockefeller saw public office as an opportunity to serve their constituents by ensuring efficient, responsible government.

The Republican rift didn't help Goldwater, who received only

39 percent of the votes in the 1964 presidential election compared with Lyndon Johnson's 61 percent. This lopsided loss had two interpretations. Many people saw it as evidence that Republicans were as out of step with the American people as their predecessors in the 1930s. An alternative view was that this peculiar assortment of antigovernment conservatives had barely begun to organize against Democrats and traditional Republicans, and yet had gotten 39 percent of the vote.

After the election, most Americans quickly put Goldwater's campaign behind them. Cynicism about Vietnam and Watergate hadn't yet taken over the national psyche. In the post–World War II era, the nation was prospering. It was time to give more Americans a shot at the American dream, and Lyndon Johnson was just the man to do it.

Lyndon Johnson's Great Society

Lyndon Baines Johnson was born in Stonewall, Texas, on August 27, 1908. He would rise from poverty to become a US congressman, US senator, senate majority leader, vice president, and after the 1963 assassination of John F. Kennedy, president of the United States. In the Senate, Johnson became the most effective legislator in American history, a talent that was largely wasted as vice president under Kennedy. But as president, he would implement a series of domestic programs second in their impact on Americans only to those of his hero, Franklin D. Roosevelt.**

Johnson's domestic policy focused on civil rights and the War on Poverty. And Lyndon Johnson certainly knew poverty. His father, Sam Johnson Jr., had been a highly regarded six-term

---

** LBJ's use of power, and the ups and downs of his career, are masterfully captured in historian Robert A. Caro's magnificent multivolume biography *The Years of Lyndon Johnson*. This is the definitive source of information on Johnson. See bibliography.

legislator in the Texas House of Representatives. But he had more success battling entrenched power in Austin than he had back home trying to earn a living by raising cattle. The Johnsons lived in the Texas Hill Country. Its poor soil and inadequate rainfall, combined with Sam Johnson's failing health, forced the family into poverty.

The Johnsons sometimes had no food in the house, and neighbors would bring them cooked meals. Women who knew the family admitted to feeling sorry for Lyndon, the tall, gangly oldest child. Lyndon would find work when he could, and this allowed him to attend Southwest Texas State Teachers College in San Marcos, about thirty miles south of Austin. Johnson participated in campus politics, where he learned to command and manipulate his peers while endearing himself to his elders. These peculiar skills and his high energy level would ensure LBJ's future political success. Johnson would learn valuable lessons early in his path to power.

In 1928, Lyndon Johnson took a year off from his studies to earn some much-needed money. He landed a job as a schoolteacher in Cotulla, a little town south of San Antonio that was more Mexican than American. Assigned to teach the poorest of the poor, Johnson was appalled by poverty worse than he himself had experienced. As the only male teacher, he was immediately appointed principal. The other five teachers at the school were local housewives who treated their jobs with indifference. Johnson labored mightily as a teacher and even introduced extracurricular activities to the school, such as debates and spelling bees. Before and after work, he tutored the school janitor in English, even paying for the man's book out of his own scarce funds.

In later years, these experiences gave Johnson the ability

to relate to the struggles of people of all races. While living in Washington, LBJ and his wife, Lady Bird, were sympathetic to the difficulties that their black servants had in finding hotel accommodations when traveling by car from Texas to the nation's capital. Yet as a Texan, Johnson would find himself naturally aligned with the Southern caucus, a voting bloc that used the Senate's arcane rules to impede attempts at desegregation in the South. As senate majority leader, however, LBJ would lead the effort to enact civil rights bills in 1957 and 1960. The bills were weak, but they were huge accomplishments given the hold that Southern segregationists had on the upper chamber of Congress.

As president, Lyndon Johnson would use his powers of persuasion to push his Great Society, domestic programs designed to improve the ability of people to survive and perhaps prosper in a modern economy. The names of these programs reverberate today as a reminder of what Americans can do to help people. In the years before the Vietnam War ate up the nation's resources, a country that readily acknowledged both its Judeo-Christian tradition and its humanity needed no explanation for why it supported LBJ's War on Poverty, Peace Corps, Job Corps, Community Action Programs, Volunteers in Service to America (VISTA), Head Start, food stamps, Medicare, and Medicaid.

Later criticisms of these programs suggested that they bred dependency. But LBJ's Great Society initiatives should be viewed as attempts to help people overcome the inadequacies of a market-based economy. As with FDR's New Deal, it was better to do something experimentally than to do nothing at all. In his five years in office, Lyndon Johnson reduced the proportion of Americans living below the poverty line from 23 percent to 12 percent, a monumental achievement.[16]

Igniting the Republican Schism

Lyndon Johnson and his Great Society had touched an egalitarian nerve. His increased use of the federal government to both enforce civil rights and improve people's economic circumstances was viewed favorably by most Americans. The tall Texan had wide support, even from what Alabama segregationist governor George Wallace called "pointy-headed" Northern liberals.

While many, perhaps most, Republicans recognized the essential humanity of Great Society programs, antigovernment extremists in the GOP were apoplectic. Republicans were also dismayed by the arithmetic of the 1964 presidential election. In 1960, Richard Nixon had effectively tied John Kennedy in the popular vote. But Barry Goldwater had lost to Johnson by a wide margin despite attracting enthusiastic new voters in both the South and the West. There was a clear explanation for this. Many Americans were appalled at both the extremism of some of Goldwater's supporters and his rigid personal views. In 1964, he had said that "extremism in the defense of liberty is no vice." In 1964, militant Black Muslim leader Malcolm X had said that "we want freedom by any means necessary."[17] The opinions of most Americans, even most Republicans, were much more moderate than those of Barry Goldwater and Malcolm X.

The 1964 election greatly magnified the existing differences in the Republican Party between a rabid antigovernment faction and more traditional conservatives. The latter, later derided as "Establishment Republicans," were willing to work in good faith to create effective public policies. But to antigovernment Republicans, "good public policy" was an oxymoron. The GOP awaited a leader who could heal, or at least minimize, this Republican schism. He would have to be someone who accepted the right-wing's ideology but was charismatic and popular enough to successfully promote a view of government that was out of step with economic reality.

Meanwhile, Lyndon Johnson seemed to be preparing a place for himself on Mount Rushmore. His domestic policies, like those of FDR, were seen as more compatible with the requirements of a modern economy than the simplistic view that markets could provide every necessity. Medicare was a much-needed Category I function of government. School desegregation was intended to help minorities get better public education, a Category III function. Food stamps and other social programs were Category IV functions, satisfying acute needs among poor people. Others, like the Peace Corps, were Category V functions, altruistic activities that reflected the essential decency of the American people. As in the 1930s, Republicans found themselves out of step with the majority of their fellow citizens. In 1964, it seemed like nothing could derail Lyndon Johnson's expanded use of the federal government.

Chapter 5
Confusion, Opportunity, and Ronald Reagan

In the years following the 1964 election, the United States would be engulfed by turmoil. The Vietnam War, Watergate, and stagflation would split the country along ideological lines, dividing families and sowing confusion in a nation whose reference point for "normality" was a postwar era characterized by national prosperity and American military dominance. Americans didn't understand that after World War II, a unique combination of pent-up demand, the birth of eighty million baby boomers, diminished foreign competition, and inherent strengths in the nation's economy had created a never-to-be-duplicated period of American history. This illusion of invincibility was shattered in the 1970s by problems both foreign and domestic. Soon after, Republicans would offer up Ronald Reagan as the nation's savior when he emerged to advocate reducing government, cutting taxes, and lessening regulation of business as the solutions to America's problems.

Foreshadowing Lyndon Johnson's Vietnam War

President Lyndon B. Johnson's domestic achievements had made him a candidate for the pantheon of great presidents: his Great Society was widely hailed as a much-needed expansion of the role that government must play in a modern economy. But in the space of just a few years, the war made him the most reviled man in America. Johnson's aggressive nature, so effective at pushing his domestic agenda, would only cause him trouble in Vietnam. This defect was evident as far back as the Cuban Missile Crisis.

In October 1962, the United States discovered that the Soviet Union was installing nuclear armed missiles in Cuba, just off the southern coast of Florida. These weapons were a threat to Miami and other American cities. President Kennedy quickly imposed a naval blockade around Cuba. He convened a task force of the nation's top leaders, including Vice President Johnson, the Joint Chiefs of Staff of the various branches of the military, Attorney General Robert Kennedy, and other top cabinet members. Lyndon Johnson and several of those present formed a hawkish faction that advocated either a preemptive air strike at Cuba or an invasion of the island. Either action could precipitate a nuclear war.

Cuban leader Fidel Castro had successfully repelled the Bay of Pigs invasion in 1961, but a much larger American attack or an airstrike might force Castro's Soviet ally to hit the nuclear button. Johnson and the other hawks were oblivious to this danger and the potential loss of millions of American lives. Rather than risk precipitating a nuclear World War III, President Kennedy and other more rational leaders sought a peaceful solution to the problem.

The impasse was resolved through diplomacy when Attorney General Robert Kennedy met secretly with the Soviet ambassador to the United States. They reached an agreement: the USSR would remove the missiles in Cuba in return for America dismantling missiles in Turkey that threatened the Soviet Union. Robert Kennedy would later say that Johnson was among a half dozen people involved in the discussions whose recommendations could have caused a nuclear catastrophe. Neither Kennedy brother believed that Johnson was fit to be president.[18]

In 1964, President Johnson would use a nebulous incident in the Tonkin Gulf to justify a dramatic expansion of military operations in Vietnam. By the time the United States lost the war in 1975, over fifty-eight thousand Americans had been killed. Johnson had left the White House in January 1969, after declining to run for reelection. Support for his administration had been undermined both by Republican opposition to his Great Society programs and by antiwar activists shouting, "Hey, hey LBJ! How many kids have you killed today?"

In the 1970s and 1980s, the protests over the war and over civil rights for blacks, Hispanics, women, and gays was a process the nation had to endure in order to achieve much-needed transformations in society. The alternative was to wait generations for changes in public opinion. The South, for example, still resisted equal rights for blacks—not surprising after centuries of slavery and racial segregation. In the short run, however, civil disobedience played into the hands of conservatives. Beginning in 1969, Republicans would occupy the White House for twenty out of the next twenty-four years.

Nixon's Fall

The Vietnam War and the turmoil it engendered brought Republican Richard M. Nixon to the White House in 1969. In the 1968 presidential campaign, Nixon had promised to use his diplomatic skills to bring the war to an end; but instead, his policies prolonged it. This intensified widespread and sometimes-violent protests that had begun in the Johnson administration. Colleges and universities, full of potential baby boomer military draftees, became focal points of antiwar sentiment. Protest songs became rallying cries for disaffected youth. John Fogerty sang, "When the band plays 'Hail to the Chief,'" they point the cannon at you." Neil Young wrote "Tin soldiers and Nixon coming" following the deaths of war protesters killed by National Guardsman at Kent State University in 1970.

America had no well-defined objective in Vietnam, and that seemed to make defeat inevitable. After the country lost the war in 1975, US Army research at the Center for Army Lessons Learned determined that the Defense Department didn't know what it was doing. It was fighting a WWII-like territorial war when a coun-terinsurgency strategy was required.[19]

This postmortem offered little consolation to a divided country. The war's strains on society and on many personal rela-tionships would last for generations. Most military personnel in Vietnam served their country well despite difficult circumstances at home and on the battlefield. But it annoyed many Americans that the "long-haired, pot-smoking hippie protesters" had been right; the war had been a waste of human life.

Like Dwight Eisenhower, Richard Nixon was not exactly the type of conservative favored by the restless right wing of the Republican Party. Nixon ended the gold standard, signed an anti-ballistic missile treaty with the Soviet Union, opened the door to diplomatic relations with Communist China, enforced desegrega-tion in Southern schools, and regulated prices to combat inflation. He expanded Category II functions of government by creating the Environmental Protection Agency and supporting numerous environmental laws, including the Clean Air Act and the Clean Water Act. Nixon also created the Occupational Safety and Health Agency (OSHA) to regulate workplace safety.

However, the Nixon administration would dissolve in scandal. First, Vice President Spiro Agnew resigned in disgrace after being charged with taking a bribe while in public office, and then Nixon himself was caught up in the Watergate fiasco. He resigned and was replaced by his new vice president, Gerald R. Ford. Then Ford was indirectly drawn into Watergate when he pardoned Nixon.

After Democrat Jimmy Carter won the 1976 presidential election, economic problems caused by the OPEC oil embargo of 1973 finally received more attention than Vietnam and Water-gate. If losing a major war to a third-world country and enduring a constitutional crisis weren't bad enough, now the economy was plagued by stagflation (high inflation, low economic output, and increasing unemployment). A befuddled nation began to ask if there was something wrong with America.

Stagflation

At the end of 1973, Arab nations incensed by American support for Israel in its October 1973 war with Egypt retaliated by dramatically increasing prices for their oil exports. These countries dominated the Organization of the Petroleum Exporting Countries (OPEC), which became their vehicle for attacking Western nations heavily dependent on petroleum imports. Oil prices rose rapidly from $2.90 a barrel in mid-1973 to $5.12 in October and $11.65 in December. Spot market prices for oil would approach $40.00 a barrel by 1981.[20] In just four years from 1973 to 1977, the oil exporters increased their earnings from $23 billion to $140 billion.[21]

Fuel prices increased dramatically in non-OPEC countries, especially in the United States, which had long been the world's leading consumer and importer of oil. In order to unravel the confusion over stagflation, it is important to understand how the impact of higher oil prices extended far beyond the price of fuel at the pump.

In the energy markets, higher oil prices caused increased prices for other fuels such as natural gas and coal. This led to higher utility costs. Businesses, especially manufacturers, often consumed huge amounts of energy so their cost of doing business soared. Since all businesses had the same problem, none of them had to worry about becoming uncompetitive by raising prices. Inflation rose dramatically, partly due to higher labor costs as some people received cost-of-living adjustments (COLA) from their employers.

The most familiar measure of inflation is the Consumer Price Index. The CPI is the annual change in average prices of a market basket of goods and services purchased by households. From 1956 through 1981, inflation in the United States was determined entirely by either the strain on resources during the Vietnam War or by the impact of rising energy costs.

In ten years (1956–1965) of gradually increased spending in Vietnam, annual inflation measured by the CPI averaged 1.64 percent. But that average jumped to 4.13 percent from 1966 to 1972 as the cost of the war exploded. It rose to 6.16 percent in 1973 as higher oil prices after the October oil embargo aggravated the problem. In 1974 and 1975, America bore the full brunt of both higher oil prices and the costs of war. Inflation averaged 10.11 percent. In 1976, the first year after the Vietnam War ended, inflation dropped to "only" 5.76 percent but rose each year to 13.58 percent in 1980, the year after a second OPEC oil embargo. From 1976 through 1981, inflation averaged 9.17 percent.[22]

Americans paid more for energy either directly (e.g., high fuel and utility prices) or indirectly (higher prices for just about everything else). This left them with less money to pay for the nonenergy component of product prices, resulting in a lower level of consumption overall. This so-called "income effect" and the end of the war caused a reduction in national output, and as a result, unemployment rose steadily, reaching 10.8 percent in the early 1980s.

Grasping at Economic Straws

What was the proper public policy response to stagflation? OPEC could raise prices and reduce the supply of oil simply by turning valves in their oil fields in a counterclockwise direction. But outside of OPEC, no one had any extra oil to make up for the shortage. President Jimmy Carter removed some regulations on oil prices, but this had no effect on world oil markets. If supply couldn't easily be increased, perhaps demand could be reduced. Americans were encouraged to carpool, drive at lower speeds, and to turn down their thermostats in winter. But the demand for energy is inelastic; i.e., the reduction in demand in response to higher prices is less than proportional to the increase in prices. Inflation steadily increased as oil prices rose.

Starting in the Carter administration, the Federal Reserve System tried to address the problem of high inflation. Standard monetary policy requires raising interest rates in response to high inflation during an economic boom. By contrast, standard monetary policy requires lowering interest rates to offset lower output and higher unemployment in a recession. But stagflation was neither a boom nor a recession. It was caused by oil embargos, factors outside the normal domestic model (i.e., by exogenous variables). Higher interest rates to combat high inflation were bound to aggravate the problems of low output and high unemployment, both of which begged for lower interest rates.

Nevertheless, Chairman Paul Volcker and the Fed instituted a tight money policy that caused interest rates to soar. In 1980, the prime rate hit 20 percent.[23] As recounted in *Secrets of the Temple*, William Greider's interesting 1987 history of the Federal Reserve System, this tight money policy was devastating to businesses and consumers alike. The cost of financing inventory or buying big-ticket items became prohibitive. By early 1981, mortgage rates exceeded 17 percent.

The Fed policy was a disaster. Volcker's arbitrary increase in interest rates could only do damage; in the second quarter of 1980, inflation-adjusted GNP shrank $39 billion and industrial production decreased by more than 8 percent. Unemployment rose from 6.3 percent in March to 7.8 percent in July as an additional 1.6 million people were put out of work.[24] The nation suffered a "double-dip" recession in 1980 and 1982. The Fed's mistake underscored two related facts: A worldwide economic problem caused by artificially high oil prices could only be solved by a significant reduction in oil prices. And lower oil prices could only come from an increase in the supply of oil from non-OPEC nations.

If the nation's leaders couldn't unravel the mysteries of stagflation, one can only imagine the general public's confusion. Inflation had spiraled upward from 1973 to 1980, and there seemed to be no solution in sight. Perhaps 95 percent of Americans were suffering. Only two groups of people benefited from high oil prices: Some people in the so-called "oil patch states" of Texas, Louisiana, and Oklahoma found themselves on the side of the economic enemy of America, OPEC, when the enemy was winning. The oil industry thrived. A second group, wealthy people with discretionary funds, could invest in oil-related companies to take advantage of the artificially high energy prices.

Stagflation had begun in the Nixon administration and grew worse under Ford. But Jimmy Carter had the misfortune of occupying the White House when the nation turned its attention from Vietnam and Watergate to its downtrodden economy. A bungled attempt in 1980 to rescue American embassy employees taken hostage in Iran only added to the sense of national misery that came to characterize Carter's four years in office. Jimmy Carter had become the Democrats' Herbert Hoover, a decent man faced with a huge and unprecedented economic problem.

Reagan to the Rescue

In 1932, the rather dour Herbert Hoover lost the presidential election by a wide margin to the effervescent Democrat Franklin

Roosevelt. In 1980, Jimmy Carter lost in a landslide to Republican Ronald Reagan, a personable former movie and television star. Reagan had been well received all over the country in 1964 when he campaigned for Barry Goldwater. That foray into politics led to Reagan's election as governor of California where he suppressed any extremist conservative tendencies while leading a very progressive state. Reagan would be the kinder, gentler face of the Republican right.

Goldwater's campaign had united various interest groups—states' righters, market purists, businessmen opposed to regulation, Southern segregationists, antitax zealots, federal land-use opponents—all of whom professed a generalized opposition to the federal government. But the 1964 election occurred before either Vietnam War spending or the first OPEC oil embargo produced massive inflation. In 1980 and beyond, however, Ronald Reagan would attempt to reshape antigovernment rhetoric to accommodate an American economy struggling with stagflation.

Reagan's economic views, later dubbed "Reaganomics," held that government wasn't the solution, it was the problem: taxes should be reduced, and markets shouldn't be fettered by government regulations. This sounded good to a confused public desperately looking for a life raft in a sea of high inflation and rising unemployment. But the phenomenon of stagflation that was devastating to America and most of the world had absolutely nothing to do with the US government, its tax policies, or its business regulations. How would Reagan's irrelevant economic policies affect very real economic problems? Ronald Reagan would take office in January 1981, and the United States would begin one of the strangest economic experiments in history.

Part II

Reaganomics as Economic Policy

Chapter 6
Morning in America

OPEC caused the global problem known as stagflation when it manipulated the oil markets and dramatically increased prices. Conservation helped, but misguided monetary policy in the United States only aggravated the nation's problems by raising interest rates. In this chapter, we will review how market forces ended stagflation and led to dramatic improvements in the American economy. Confusion about this period in economic history still distorts public policy discussions in America today.

Stagflation could only be ended by increases in non-OPEC oil production, and the oil industry would eventually deliver it. But the market response took more time than anyone, even economists, ever expected.

A Long-Term Correction
Every economist knows how markets respond to a significant increase in the price of a product. Producers increase output to take advantage of the opportunity to make higher profits. The proverbial widget manufacturers, for example, might run their widget assembly lines for longer periods of time, perhaps adding another shift of workers at night or on the weekend. They increase production now in response to today's higher prices.

But it is not always possible to rev up production of a product quickly to take advantage of higher prices. If, for example, cattle ranchers reduce their herds in a period of drought, beef prices may soar. But even when the rains return, it may take two or three years to increase herd sizes and fatten cattle in order to take advantage of the higher beef prices.

Unfortunately, oil producers operate on an even longer time

frame than cattle producers. As a result, markets didn't seem to be very responsive to higher oil prices in the 1970s and early 1980s. To most people, oil markets mean either daily sales on the so-called spot market or perhaps the sale of contracts for transactions a few months or a year or two into the future. But oil producers around the world had no extra production to bring to market when OPEC started raising prices. Economists would have to take a broader and more long-term view of oil markets to include the search for new oil fields.

Exploration and Production

Finding new oil reserves can take years. First, exploration geologists and geophysicists acquire and analyze scientific data, looking for a good place for engineers to drill an exploratory or "wildcat" well. If they find a desirable drilling location (and frequently they do not), then their company must acquire mineral rights to the acreage. If there is competition for this land or offshore block, this process can take many months. If the wildcat well appears to be economically productive (and sometimes it is not), then the oil company may drill one or more additional wells to further delineate the extent of the underground reservoir. If the reservoir is large enough to justify additional investment, then surface production equipment and a pipeline will be constructed. Only then can the oil be sold.

Oil and natural gas from producing wells flow from beneath the ground 24/7, gradually depleting subsurface reservoirs. So oil companies must have a certain amount of successful exploration just to replace the reserves being drained every day. But beginning with the 1973 OPEC oil embargo, the worldwide oil industry was faced with both an opportunity and a problem. Oil prices rose from about $3.00 a barrel in early 1973 to nearly $40.00 a barrel in

1981, so there were certainly profits to be made. The problem was the need for incremental production; that is, additional production beyond that necessary to replace depleting reservoirs. It would take years to hire and train the extra people needed to begin the multiyear projects that would increase the world's oil supply and reduce high OPEC prices.

The effort to increase the geophysical staff at a regional office of Amoco Production Company, a major oil company, illustrates the problems the oil industry had in expanding its exploration and production capabilities. Just after the October 1973 oil embargo, the office had sixty geophysicists. By the end of 1980, the company had increased the number of geophysicists to 120. It accomplished this despite the fact that during those seven years, eighty-four geophysicists were transferred to other company offices or hired by competitors. Thus the net gain of sixty required adding 144 new geophysicists (60 + 84), all but five of whom came straight from college.[25] Training these new college graduates became a major project for large oil companies that were losing experienced people regularly to smaller E & P companies.

The rather confusing delay in the response to OPEC's interference in oil markets was due to both the long-term nature of E & P projects and the need for companies to increase staff in order to find incremental production. The American oil industry was quick to defend itself against charges of windfall profits but didn't take time to explain the long-term market response.

Economists unfamiliar with E & P couldn't understand what was happening. As a result, there were many politically motivated explanations for the turnaround in the American economy in the 1980s, a turnaround that was entirely due to the reduction in oil prices caused by increased worldwide production. In later chapters, we'll see how those politically motivated explanations lingered long after markets finished correcting the problem of stagflation.

Geology and the American Market Response

American companies made significant contributions to finding extra oil production after the 1973 embargo. But we have to know a little geology to understand why most of their larger oil discoveries were either outside the lower forty-eight states or in foreign countries.

Both oil and natural gas are hydrocarbons. Natural gas can be thought of as oil that has been buried deeper in the ground and kept at higher temperatures, effectively cooked from a liquid into a gas. Thus oil deposits tend to be shallower than natural gas deposits.

In the mid–nineteenth century, the industry only had the technology to drill very shallow wells for crude oil, a valuable substitute for the increasingly scarce whale oil used in lamps. The first oil well in America was famously drilled in 1859 by Col. Edwin L. Drake in Titusville, Pennsylvania. Drake found oil production at a depth of only seventy feet beneath the surface. After that, wildcatters drilled all over the country for oil, sometimes discovering huge fields.[26]

There were plenty of substitute food products for whale meat. But for generations, whale oil was particularly well suited for oil lamps. Thanks to the successful new drilling in the United States after Drake's discovery, whale oil was no longer needed for illumination. Much to the shock of early environmentalists, the oil industry did more than anyone else to save the whales.

Petroleum is a finite, nonrenewable resource. Even before 1973, the year of the first OPEC oil embargo, it was hard to find additional economical quantities of crude oil in the United States;

new domestic drilling was increasingly for natural gas. So American companies largely had to go overseas to find oil production. A major exception was the 1967 discovery by Atlantic Richfield (ARCO) and Humble Refining (EXXON) of Prudhoe Bay Field in Alaska. After the Trans-Alaska Pipeline System was completed in 1977, this giant field became America's major contribution to offset the oil shortage. By 1978, it was producing more than one million barrels a day. Within a few years, production was increased to two million barrels a day.[27] Prudhoe Bay was discovered before the first oil embargo, but higher prices afterward made development and pipeline construction economical.

Parenthetically, our explanation of how E & P works helps us understand the significance of shale fracking, a technology that has recently received lots of attention. Before fracking, the industry couldn't produce from shallow rock formations called shale, which were known to contain oil. Shale has plenty of porosity, or open spaces, to hold oil. But shale lacks permeability, the connections between the porosity necessary for oil to flow to the surface. For generations, the oil industry had drilled through shale formations but lacked the technology to exploit them. Then the fracking process was developed to create permeability by using high-pressure injection of both fluids and solids to shatter the shale. After 2007, the success of shale fracking in the United States would dramatically lower energy costs and completely change the world's oil markets.

Japan Thrives; America Lags
From 1950 to 1990, Japan had the highest economic growth of any country in the history of the world up to that point.[28] The Japanese even prospered through the 1973 to 1981 period of dramatically increasing oil prices despite the fact that they had

to import almost all their oil. But the United States had a large domestic oil industry and still suffered mightily from stagflation.

The contrast between the countries' fortunes and the confusion about the long-term market response led to much ideologically based speculation. In the United States, antigovernment conservatives claimed that the relative decline in America's economy was due to the cumulative impact of big government programs. Surely, FDR's New Deal and LBJ's Great Society were to blame for high inflation and high unemployment. The Japanese didn't need welfare; they just rolled up their sleeves and worked.

The true explanation reveals something different. The problem didn't lie with the provision of government services resulting from well-known market inadequacies, as described in chapter 1. In his fascinating history of the oil industry, *The Prize: The Epic Quest for Oil, Money, and Power*, Daniel Yergin explains that in Japan, companies, unions, and individuals worked together with their government to conserve energy and lessen dependence on expensive oil imports. They curtailed the use of elevators, experimented with wearing short-sleeve jackets to reduce the need for air-conditioning in the summer, switched to other forms of energy like coal and natural gas, and began to consciously emphasize "knowledge-intensive" industry rather than "energy-intensive" industry. The energy shock and widespread cooperation forced rapid and permanent changes in Japanese industry.[29]

By contrast, proposals for conservation in the United States were often met with opposition from market purists who were more concerned with the government telling people what to do than about reducing oil imports and stemming the flow of dollars overseas. Yet under Republican president Gerald Ford, the nation managed to overcome this ideologically motivated resistance and pass legislation in 1975 that mandated automobile fuel efficiency

standards. The same legislation established a strategic petroleum reserve, an idea that had originated with President Eisenhower. These two government functions would, respectively, save
America money on oil imports and increase energy security.[30]

Such cooperation between Americans and their government
had worked well to win World War II. Yet market purists continued
to resist federal efforts to overcome oil embargos that some
people called the economic equivalent of war. America still suffers
today from conflicts between good public policy and ideological
purity.

The Battle for Market Share

After the first oil embargo in 1973, non-OPEC countries and
companies intensified their search for new oil reserves. New
production entered the market from all over the world. High oil
prices allowed the rapid development of newly discovered fields
like Prudhoe Bay in Alaska. The OPEC countries would eventually
struggle to maintain market share as they increasingly had to
compete with cheaper crude sold daily on the spot market.

In *The Prize*, Yergin describes the dramatic increase in world
oil production that would ultimately undermine OPEC's market
dominance.[31] In 1969, Phillips Petroleum of Bartlesville, Oklahoma, made a huge oil discovery in the North Sea between Great
Britain and Norway. High oil prices accelerated development of
what would become the single-largest contributor to incremental
world oil production in the 1970s and early 1980s. Production
that began in the British sector in 1975 would eventually reach 2.5
million barrels of oil a day. In 1983, the North Sea produced more
than three major OPEC nations combined: Algeria, Libya, and
Nigeria. By 1985, output from the British sector alone exceeded
that of the biggest OPEC producer, Saudi Arabia.

It may seem suspicious that oil prices soared after the first OPEC oil embargo just in time to finance the expensive development of two new American-operated oil fields, Prudhoe Bay and the North Sea. But no one has ever shown any collusion between OPEC and these American companies.

New discoveries by PEMEX in the 1970s would also make Mexico a major oil exporter. Mexican output surged from 500,000 barrels a day in 1973 to 830,000 barrels a day in 1976. Production would reach 1.9 million barrels by 1980. By the early to mid-1980s, Alaska, Mexico, and the North Sea would add six to seven million barrels of oil per day to the world oil markets. New production even came from unexpected sources such as Egypt, Malaysia, Angola, and China, all of which became oil exporters.

OPEC nations lost market share when their customers deserted them and bought cheaper oil from other countries. In a hastily arranged meeting in March 1983, OPEC oil ministers agreed to lower their prices by about 15 percent, from thirty-nine to thirty-four dollars a barrel. However, this oil price concession wouldn't be enough.

High oil prices since 1973 had depressed economic activity in many non-OPEC countries. Lower demand combined with conservation to reduce oil consumption in the non-Communist world by six million barrels a day from 1979 to 1983. Battered by both reduced demand and increased supply, the cartel began to collapse.* OPEC's biggest exporter, Saudi Arabia, tried to act as

---

*   In order to maintain its high oil prices, the OPEC cartel had established an export quota system (an "embargo" from the importers' viewpoint) among its members to keep them from flooding the markets. But cheating was rampant as OPEC countries succumbed to the temptation of high prices. This played a role in the increased worldwide output that ended the cartel's grip on petroleum markets; but by far the biggest sources of extra oil production were Prudhoe Bay, the North Sea, and increased output from Mexico.

a swing producer and reduce its output. Saudi production that had once been 10 million barrels a day fell to 2.2 million by 1985. This yielded revenue of only $26 billion, a far cry from 1981 when Saudi Arabia earned $119 billion.

Dismayed by their loss of market share, the Saudis finally threw up their hands in disgust. In 1985, they lowered their prices and began to increase production. World oil prices collapsed. In the United States, the benchmark price for West Texas intermediate-grade (WTI) crude oil fell from a peak of $31.75 a barrel in November 1985 to only $10.00 a few years later.

OPEC learned a hard lesson: markets work! OPEC nations had made hundreds of billions of extra dollars by colluding to raise oil prices in the 1970s, only to lose revenue in the 1980s as newly discovered oil seemed to come out of the woodwork. In the future, they would adhere to market-determined prices and hold on to their share of the market. In 2014, increases in world oil production from hugely successful shale-fracking efforts in the United States caused WTI's benchmark price to decline from $107 a barrel to less than $50. A big factor in the dramatic price reduction was Saudi Arabia's announcement that it would emphasize maintaining market share rather than reducing exports.

The End of Stagflation

The collapse of oil prices in the 1980s effectively reversed the process that had caused stagflation and economic misery in the 1970s. Lower oil prices caused a reduction in the costs of competing forms of energy like natural gas and coal. This dramatically reduced inflation. Cost-of-living adjustments were no longer necessary and that, in turn, stabilized labor costs. Less spending on energy put more money in the pockets of consumers, who could then spend more on things other than energy. Greater consumption led to increased output by businesses that were also enjoying the lower cost of energy. The higher output required new workers, which reduced unemployment.

The Federal Reserve Bank's disastrous tight money policy had raised interest rates. This had caused recessions in both 1980 and 1982. But lower inflation after the collapse of oil prices in the 1980s began to put downward pressure on interest rates. It became much easier for businesses to finance inventory and investment. Consumers could more easily borrow money to buy big-ticket items like houses, cars, and appliances.

The US economy had steadily gotten worse in the period from the first OPEC embargo in 1973 to 1982, a year in which unemployment peaked at 10.8 percent. But things improved rapidly as market forces brought down energy prices. Inflation fell from 13.5 percent in 1980 to 4.1 percent in 1988.[32] GDP growth went from negative 0.3 percent in 1980 to positive 4.1 percent in 1988.[33] Annual job growth averaged 2.1 percent from 1981 through 1988. Unemployment that had averaged 6.4 percent in the late 1970s fell to only 5.4 percent by the end of the 1980s.[34] Paul Volcker's tight money policy caused the prime interest rate, the rate banks charge to their best customers, to soar to an average of 14.1 percent between 1979 and 1984. But as inflation declined, the prime rate followed suit, averaging 8.9 percent from 1985 through 1988.[35] Market forces had worked beautifully to negate the impact of OPEC's interference in the oil markets.

It was morning in America!

Chapter 7
Reaganomics

It had taken them sixteen years to do it, but in 1980 the Republican Party finally won the 1964 presidential election. The new president, Ronald Reagan, was much more appealing to voters than the stern, uncompromising Barry Goldwater. Reagan's plans to reduce public sector spending, cut taxes, and minimize regulation were shaped by Goldwater's antigovernment views. But as we saw in the previous chapter, Reagan's economic policy, Reaganomics, was absolutely irrelevant to the corrections in the world oil markets that brought an end to the stagflation and economic misery that helped get Reagan elected.

Everyone, especially conservatives, could proudly proclaim that markets had worked extremely well to reduce inflation and spur both higher output and greater employment. But if Reaganomics had nothing to do with the dramatic improvements in the American economy during the 1980s, then what *was* the impact of Reagan's economic policies during his eight years in the White House?

The Savings and Loan Crisis

The Federal Reserve System's misguided tight money policy that began in the late 1970s was a disaster for most consumers and businesses. High interest rates made financing any kind of purchase extremely difficult, and company profits suffered as a result. An analysis of Federal Reserve data by economist Gerald Epstein indicated that in the 1979 to 1982 period, the pretax profits of nonfinancial corporations averaged 10.7 percent, a huge decline from the long-term average of 15.9 percent from 1960 to 1978. But commercial banks thrived. Their return on equity from

1979 to 1982 averaged 13.2 percent, well above their long-term average of 10.4 percent.[36]

Not all financial institutions were so fortunate, however. Savings and loan associations held portfolios of long-term mortgages at low interest rates. But the Fed's new policy forced them to pay high interest to attract depositors. To make matters worse, few people could afford to finance home purchases at mortgage interest rates that approached 17 percent. The S&Ls needed help with a problem that was not of their own making, but that help would not come from the Reagan administration.

A market purist, Ronald Reagan didn't believe in government solutions to problems in the markets, even when the problems were caused by Federal Reserve policy. With Reaganomics as his template, Reagan selected deregulation as his response. This, despite the fact that government regulations had nothing at all to do with the S&Ls' problems. After Reagan's deregulation, the thrifts' only means of escape was to try to use their newly granted commercial lending ability to make money. But they were specialists in home mortgage lending and had no expertise in commercial loans.

"Developers" of nebulous projects who could not get loans from experienced commercial lenders flocked to savings and loan companies. All across the country, S&Ls began to lend money for apartment complexes, office buildings, and retail stores. After just a few years of wild and irresponsible lending, the savings and loan industry destroyed itself as one foolish loan after another began to sour. An incredible 1,645 out of 3,234 S&Ls would disappear between 1986 and 1995.[37]

In the "real economy" (i.e., the nonfinancial sector), businesses are allowed to go bankrupt all the time without any government intervention. But if a financial institution goes under, part of the money supply of the United States could disappear. So the Federal Savings and Loan Insurance Corporation had been created in 1934 to insure most S&L deposits (banks are insured by the FDIC). In the 1980s, the US government suddenly found itself taking over numerous failed S&Ls.

So many absurd commercial loans had been made after Reagan's deregulation that the federal government had to do something to resolve hundreds of billions of dollars in defaults held by insolvent financial institutions. Often these loans were backed by apartment complexes, office buildings, and other commercial properties that should never have been built. Somehow, these physical properties had to be maintained and disposed of.

The Resolution Trust Corporation (RTC), which began operations on January 1, 1989, was created by the federal government to systematically liquidate these and other S&L assets. By 1990 the RTC had $210 billion in assets, more than any other corporation in America. Its assets included "shopping malls, junk bonds, two-thirds of the thrift assets of the state of Arizona, and a piece of the Dallas Cowboys."[38] A mindless commitment to market purity had exacerbated a private sector problem that then required a government solution. Ultimately this disaster would be dumped in the lap of Reagan's successor, George H. W. Bush.

Leveraged Buyouts

Investment bankers are in the business of doing deals, any kind of deals, as long as they can make money. They are not in the business of building companies, not even their own; they don't want stock options, they want cash. Having someone in the White House gullible enough to oppose regulation is an opportunity to be exploited. Without adequate government oversight, even sensible business strategies can explode into problems. During the Reagan administration, inadequate regulation would combine with the collapse of oil prices to create both chaos and opportunities for profits.

Oilman T. Boone Pickens saw an opportunity during the 1980s. Pickens is a rare individual, both a good geologist and a good businessman. Accounting rules require oil companies to "write down," or reduce, the asset value of oil and natural gas reserves on their balance sheets when lower prices make some reserves uneconomical to produce. But Pickens knew that the underlying assets didn't disappear and, in fact, would likely regain their value when higher prices returned. This loss of asset value had combined with reduced revenue to dramatically depress oil company stock prices in the 1980s. As the chairman of Mesa Petroleum, Pickens recognized that it made more sense to buy companies and wait out the oil markets than to look for new oil reserves. This strategy came to be called "finding oil on the balance sheet."

At various times between 1982 and 1985, Pickens bought stock in Cities Service, Gulf Oil, Phillips Petroleum, and Union Oil of California (UNOCAL).[39] He could use so-called "junk bonds," or high-interest debt, and the target company's own assets to finance these big stock purchases. Pickens soon found out that entrenched management in these companies didn't want to be bought out and would pay him a premium price to get out of their hair. When Pickens profited enormously from this so-called "greenmail," his success did not go unnoticed on Wall Street.

Ever opportunistic, investment bankers realized that they could use Pickens's strategy to attempt a takeover of just about any company. Leveraged buyout (LBO) deals proliferated on Wall Street and companies that feared takeovers began to neglect normal business activities. Some corporate executives schemed to buy out their own employers, take the company private, and profit from efficiency measures that they had previously neglected. For a few years during the Reagan administration, chaos reigned in the corporate world. Gibson Greetings (1982), TWA (1985), Revco (1986), Federated Department Stores (1988), and other companies were taken over by outside entities, often against the wishes of entrenched management. The chaos only stopped when federal investigators prosecuted key figures for illegal insider trading.

The LBO problem wasn't nearly as costly to the nation as the S&L crisis, but it offered a more valuable lesson. Business regulation is a critical Category II function of government, and if it's neglected, the financial sector can act rapidly and on a massive scale to create huge problems that damage the entire nation.

Tax Cuts

When he took office in 1981, Ronald Reagan acted quickly to reduce federal income taxes. Many Americans had received cost-of-living adjustments (COLAs) from their employers to help them combat inflation after the 1973 oil embargo. In a progressive tax system, this had moved them into higher tax brackets. Some tax relief was certainly justified, particularly for lower- and middle-income wage earners.

But this created a problem. Many of Reagan's supporters had the impression that there was something inherently good about cutting taxes and using borrowed money to pay the bills. This would only increase the national debt. That problem was compounded by the fact that Reagan's tax cuts tended to disproportionately favor the wealthy. As we'll see in chapter 14, this only increases certain types of transactions, whether for consumption or investment, that tend to diminish employment.

As we noted in chapter 2, taxation is simply a consequence of federal government spending. Market inadequacies are remedied by government actions that are paid for with tax revenue. In other words, we have to pay taxes because we have a market economy. There is, therefore, no rational basis for any general opposition to taxation. Tax revenue is good because it pays the bills. Paying taxes is bad only because getting things "free" is typically seen as preferable to paying for them. But Reagan's supporters pointed to the famous Kennedy tax cuts in the 1960s as the prototype for beneficial tax relief.

Beginning in the 1940s, the nation had imposed high personal and corporate tax rates on itself to cover the huge costs of World War II. When Lyndon Johnson became president following the assassination of John Kennedy, the highest marginal rate on personal income stood at 90 percent. But tax revenue is determined by both the rate of taxation and the level of taxable income, and the latter had increased during the country's postwar boom. Walter Heller and other liberal economists in the Kennedy administration had suggested that this higher taxable income would allow a reduction in income tax rates and that, in turn, would further spur the economy.

In 1964, LBJ eagerly embraced Heller's proposal and applied his own considerable powers of persuasion to push tax cut legislation through Congress. But Johnson had to overcome opposition from congressional conservatives suspicious of Heller's liberal tax cut idea. After all, there was nothing more conservative than fiscal responsibility. If a country didn't keep tight control of its debts, unexpected events such as war or a recession could cause debt to spiral out of control. Also, current unpaid bills would become an unfair burden to future generations.

In the 1980s, Ronald Reagan's followers effectively flipped

the ideological spectrum 180 degrees. Emanating from the most conservative faction of the Republican Party, tax reduction would be wielded as a weapon against government. But, as noted before, taxation is simply a consequence of government spending that is determined by needs not met by the private sector. Cutting taxes cannot make the needs go away.

The US economy would improve after the collapse of oil prices described in chapter 6, so it was possible that increases in taxable income could offset the Reagan administration's reductions in tax rates. But this delicate balance could be undermined by any lack of fiscal restraint.

Star Wars, Increased Defense Spending, and Budget Deficits

During the Carter administration, Republicans had complained that decreased military spending had weakened the nation. Defense spending reached 10 percent of GDP at the height of the Vietnam War in 1968 and fell to 6 percent of GDP in the mid-1970s. Under Jimmy Carter, it hit a low of 5.5 percent of GDP in 1979.[40] But these numbers can only be properly understood in their historical context.

Most of the reduction in military spending can be attributed to the decline in American troops in Vietnam. At its peak, the United States had a force of five hundred thousand soldiers in Southeast Asia. This was reduced to zero after the United States pulled out of Vietnam in 1975. Defense contractors didn't need to provide equipment to former soldiers who had gone home to their families. Military preparedness is important, but peace costs a lot less than war.

Americans had developed a taste for military spending during World War II when the Defense Department's budget hit 40 percent of GDP. For decades after the war, communities across the country loved obsolete postwar military installations that provided employment for servicemen and local civilians. For some reason, this wasteful government spending was deemed to be a better use of public funds than food stamps that kept people from starving, Medicaid that kept people from dying, or education and training that kept the nation economically competitive.

It was fortunate that during the 1980s, America's primary Cold War enemy was occupied with problems of its own. The collapse of oil prices that had revived the US economy was devastating to the Soviet Union. The Soviets depended on oil exports for most of their hard currency and quickly found it impossible to support their far-flung empire.

Weak allies like Cuba would suffer from permanent reductions in Soviet aid, while satellite countries in Europe like Poland and East Germany would become increasingly restless. The USSR had become bogged down in a war in Afghanistan in 1979, the year before Ronald Reagan took office, and was preoccupied by that expensive and deadly war throughout the Reagan years.

So why were American conservatives complaining about less military spending? The end of the Vietnam War and a weaker Soviet Union should have been welcome news to Republicans who wanted to reduce both government and taxes. But this opportunity for less government was overwhelmed by complaints from politically influential defense contractors with nothing to do. So Reagan quickly revved up his Strategic Defense Initiative program, popularly known as Star Wars. This and other peacetime military spending soon increased the nation's defense budget from 5.5 percent of GDP in the Carter administration to a high of 6.8 percent of GDP in 1986 under Reagan.[41]

Reagan's increased defense spending didn't mix well with his tax cuts. Budget deficits soared and by 1990 were triple the deficit in 1980, the last year of the Carter administration. Reagan had created the biggest peacetime deficits in American history. To straighten out the disaster, he raised taxes numerous times and borrowed more and more money. Under Ronald Reagan, the United States ceased to be the world's largest creditor nation and became instead the world's largest debtor nation.[42]

When Reagan took office in January 1981, he declared that the federal budget was "out of control." The national debt was $930 billion. By the end of 1988, his last full year in the White House, the debt totaled $2.6 trillion. Looking back on the Reagan years, economic historian J. Bradford DeLong wrote that, "The tax cuts made America a more unequal place, and the deficits slowed economic growth in the 1980s significantly."[43]

Reaganomics was a rather strange application of capitalism: it capitalized on the widespread confusion in America over both the cause and the cure of stagflation, and the misery that peculiar economic phenomenon had inflicted on the country. Republicans had fallen into a political advantage that was not of their own making. But it should have occurred to most people that Reaganomics was an attempt to defy economic reality.

Under Ronald Reagan, America's greater military strength came at the expense of increased economic weakness. Reagan had been extraordinarily lucky; lower oil prices had simultaneously helped the US economy and weakened the nation's biggest enemy. But excessive tax cuts and his commitment to deregulation had yielded both big budget deficits and turmoil in the financial sector. When you're lucky and fail, it's time to reconsider your economic policies.

Every day of their lives, Americans depend for their very survival on the fact that Reaganomics is nonsense. The need for public infrastructure, national defense, police protection, health regulations, Medicare, Social Security, and many other government functions should not be dismissed just because an appealing politician came along in a moment of confusion and said things that people thought they wanted to hear.

Chapter 8
Better Lucky Than Good: 1981–2000

Reaganomics always fails as economic policy; it is an attempt to defy the requirements of a modern economy that we described in chapter 1. But because of the disaster that began in early 2001, the eight years that Reagan was in office and the next twelve years under George H. W. Bush and Bill Clinton are remembered as a time of relative economic prosperity. This only added to the confusion of an American public that still thought that in some vague and undefined way, Reaganomics had ended stagflation in the 1980s.

Further confusion stems from the fact that there is no "normal" in American economic history, only a series of ups and downs in the economy. So people eagerly assume that the last period of prosperity must have been the "normal" economy they desire. The notion that another downturn may be in the offing only adds stress to lives that may already be difficult.

The roaring twenties gave way to the Great Depression when excessive debt, unrestrained speculation on Wall Street, and natural disasters buried the nation in economic misery. Nearly four years of sacrifices in World War II helped save the world and finished the economic recovery begun by the New Deal. The United States became the dominant economic and military power at a time in which there was little competition. Other countries were either recovering from the war or still had undeveloped economies. The "American dream" was formed in this peculiar era of little global competition, pent-up postwar demand, and the birth of eighty million baby boomers.

When the bubble was burst by Vietnam, Watergate, oil

embargos, stagflation, the rise of Japan, and the Iranian hostage crisis, Ronald Reagan came along and invoked memories of postwar prosperity. Stagflation helped get Reagan elected the first time; the market correction that ended stagflation was timed perfectly to get him reelected. If the correction had occurred earlier, it might have gotten Jimmy Carter reelected. Since the economy was initially worse under Reagan than under Carter, a delay in the market correction might have cost Reagan the presidency in 1984. Incredibly, Ronald Reagan's luck in economic matters extended to foreign policy.

Reagan and Gorbachev

Ronald Reagan's foreign policy concerns were greatly simplified by circumstances beyond his control. America's principal enemy in the world was tied up in a major war that began before he became president and ended after he left office. The USSR had invaded Afghanistan in 1979 to support an unpopular Communist government. Following a period of initial success, the Soviets finally lost the war in 1989 after the United States supplied the opposition Mujahedeen forces with shoulder-mounted, heat-seeking missile launchers. The missiles, provided by the CIA at the behest of Democratic East Texas congressman Charlie Wilson, were very effective against the helicopter gunships that had initially given the Soviets military superiority.

Reagan's luck didn't end there. The market-driven collapse in oil prices in the 1980s that ended stagflation was devastating to the Soviet Union. Moscow depended on revenue from oil exports to support Communist regimes all over the world. Many were dependent on the USSR to overcome their inefficient economic systems. But market forces in the capitalist world (see chapter 6) caused the evil empire to run out of money.

Many people in the Soviet Socialist Republics remembered their glory days as independent nations. By the 1980s, they were united only by a common desire to free themselves from the Kremlin. When the natives became restless and protested in the streets in Poland and East Germany, Moscow didn't have the resources or the desire to intervene. Its military was tied up in Afghanistan, and many Soviet citizens were dismayed at the increasing numbers of body bags and injured soldiers returning home from war.

To complicate matters, many younger Soviets enjoyed rock and roll, blue jeans, and other aspects of American and British culture and had little sympathy for their elders' Cold War–style animosity toward the West. But the end of the Soviet Union would begin when the triple disasters of Afghanistan, low oil prices, and changing attitudes were dropped in the lap of a middle-age Russian quite unlike any leader the nation had ever seen before.

Mikhail Gorbachev became the leader of the Soviet Union in March 1985, after his three aging predecessors died in office. The deaths, all apparently from natural causes, of Leonid Brezhnev (1982), Yuri Andropov (1984), and Konstantin Chernenko (1985) signaled the changing of the guard in the Kremlin. These fossils had been nurtured during the brutal regime of Joseph Stalin. They were replaced by a new type of Soviet leader, one with a more realistic view of the limitations of the Communist state.

Like other rising stars in the Soviet system, Mikhail Gorbachev had shown both leadership ability and a devotion to Communism. His training prepared him for increased responsibilities in a system that, according to his instructors, was far ahead of the West. But when he and many of his carefully selected contemporaries visited Soviet embassies abroad, they discovered that they had been lied to. Economically, the West was far ahead of the Soviet Union. After assuming power in Moscow, Gorbachev would attempt to both restructure the Communist system and allow more openness in Soviet society.

For a few years after Ronald Reagan took office in 1981, Soviet leaders were dying off too fast to become targets of the famous Reagan charm offensive. But he and Mikhail Gorbachev got along just fine, if only because they were united by a shared belief: their countries were wasting massive resources building nuclear weapons whose sole purpose was to destroy the world. This led to the 1987 Intermediate-Range Nuclear Forces (INF) Treaty. The INF Treaty was the first agreement between the two Cold War powers designed to actually reduce nuclear arsenals instead of just stabilizing them at high levels.[44] This would be Reagan's only significant achievement. It would also save both countries a lot of money.

The Soviets' savings on missiles would not be enough to overcome the devastating effects of low oil prices. Economic problems, Afghanistan, and unchecked dissension in satellite countries would lead to the collapse of the Soviet Union in 1991. The presence of Mikhail Gorbachev and other cool heads in the Kremlin assured that no one pushed the nuclear button in frustration as the Communists lost the Cold War.

Republicans promoted the notion that Reagan's famous 1987 speech at the Berlin Wall had led to the demise of the Soviet Union. "Mr. Gorbachev, tear down this wall" was one of the many theatrical moments that highlighted Reagan's eight years in office. Supposedly, the Kremlin leaders read a Russian translation of the speech and declared it to be so impressive that they had to disband their empire. Among American conservatives, the myth that Ronald Reagan defeated the Soviet Union joined the myth that Reaganomics had somehow saved the United States from stagflation.

Skeptics and Loyal Soldiers

Many Republicans were skeptical of Reaganomics, including George Herbert Walker Bush, Ronald Reagan's main competitor for the 1980 Republican presidential nomination. In the view of right-wing Goldwater Republicans like Reagan, Bush represented the wrong wing of the party—moderates who had been ineffective for decades in stemming the Democratic Party's expansion of government. The 1980 primary was just one of many increasingly bitter battles between the two warring factions in the Republican Party.

In a speech at Carnegie Mellon University on April 10, 1980, Bush became the nation's most prominent critic of Reaganomics. He referred to Reagan's proposed economic policies as "voodoo economics."[45] But Bush wasn't the only Republican expressing skepticism about Reagan's plans to cut taxes while increasing defense spending.

During the 1980 campaign, the Reagan camp had approached David Stockman, a highly regarded young Republican congressman from Michigan considered to be an expert on the national budget. But Stockman was supporting former Texas Democratic governor John Connally, now running for president as a Republican. Stockman had determined that the theory behind Reaganomics was flawed. According to Stockman, if Reagan went ahead with his tax cuts and defense spending increases, the only way to avoid huge budget deficits would be to implement deep reductions in domestic programs.[46]

But Americans relied on government to make up for inadequacies in the private sector. Even the most ardent conservatives recognized that government functions satisfy important needs while creating valuable jobs that would not otherwise exist. For example, Republican congressman Jack Kemp, a stalwart supporter of Reagan's policies, rejected excessive spending cuts. Kemp represented Buffalo, New York, an urban area where many jobs were tied to government programs.[47]

After Reagan won the GOP nomination, he selected Bush to be his vice presidential running mate. This allowed him to lock in the support of Bush's moderate Republican followers. It also eliminated the possibility that as president, Reagan would have to put up with a prominent Republican critic complaining about "voodoo economics."

Stockman was appointed Reagan's budget director after the election. But in a series of interviews with William Greider of the *Atlantic Monthly* magazine between December 1980 and September 1981, Stockman expressed skepticism about Reagan's policies. He said that "there was a certain dimension of our theory that was unrealistic." Stockman referred to the proposed across-the-board tax cuts as "trickle-down economics" because they disproportionately benefited the wealthy. According to his biographer, Owen Ullmann, Stockman conceded that "his initial budget numbers were constructed on shaky premises" and that ultimately, "defense numbers got out of control."[48]

In the view of many prominent Republicans, the Reagan Revolution was over before it had even begun. Sure enough, Reagan's failure to adequately regulate the financial sector produced the S&L crisis and the leveraged buyout problems on Wall Street. And as David Stockman had predicted, tax cuts plus increased defense spending caused huge budget deficits. In the 1980 election, Ronald Reagan had asked Americans if they were better off under Jimmy Carter than under Gerald Ford. But in the early 1980s, Americans were worse off under Reagan than under Carter. Even after market corrections in the mid-1980s eliminated stagflation (chapter 6), there were so many problems caused by

Reagan's policies that most Americans never seemed to get the full benefit of an improving economy. The exceptions, of course, were wealthy Americans who had received big tax cuts.

Number Forty-One

After George H. W. Bush defeated Democrat Michael Dukakis in 1988, his main task as president was to clean up the Reaganomics disaster that he had all but predicted in 1980. On Wall Street, a series of investigations would bring stability after years of turmoil. Junk bond king Michael Milken and prominent arbitrager Ivan Boesky would go to prison.

Also under Bush, the assets of dissolved savings and loan associations were put into the newly created Resolution Trust Corporation. The RTC would attempt to find a graceful way to unload apartment complexes and office buildings constructed after Reagan's deregulation policies had permitted, and in some ways even encouraged, foolish lending practices.

A bigger problem for Bush was the budget deficits that resulted from years of increased defense spending and inadequate taxation under Reagan. Bush had appeased the Republican right wing with a "no new taxes" pledge in the 1988 election. But the Democratic-controlled Congress and most Americans opposed balancing the budget with cuts in vital government programs that were needed to make up for deficiencies in the marketplace. When Bush broke his pledge and raised taxes, so-called Reagan Republicans never forgave him. They offered him only lukewarm support in the 1992 election and he lost to Democrat Bill Clinton. Bush acted responsibly and became a one-term president. Reagan's economic policies failed, but forces beyond his control made him a two-term president. In politics, sometimes it's indeed better to be lucky than good.

Reagan Republicans and Bush had policy differences going back to the 1980 Republican nomination fight. But Bush's loss in the 1992 election and the prospect of another Democrat in the White House would be the beginning of the end for moderate Republicans. Henceforth, they would be reduced to minimizing disruptive tactics by the GOP's right wing while trying to exert some influence over its increasingly extremist policies.

Bush had stood his ground against the antitax, antigovernment faction in his own party and had kept Reagan's budget deficits from spiraling out of control. As a decorated Navy pilot in World War II, Bush had known men who later died while fighting for America. He wasn't going to let a bunch of hotheads—even Republican hotheads—wreck his country's finances over something as comparatively trivial as tax cuts for the rich. His courage would not be recognized until 2014 when he was awarded the Kennedy Profile in Courage award.[49] By then, the nation had tasted more than three decades of Reagan's failed economic policies and was sorely in need of another George H. W. Bush.

Breaking Bad: The Republicans in Opposition

In 1993, Reagan Republicans were appalled that another Democrat, Bill Clinton, was in the White House. This wasn't supposed to happen and called for an intensified attack on government. To be clear, their hostility wasn't directed at the Iranian government, the Chinese government, or the North Korean government. Like Goldwater conservatives in the 1960s, their enemy was the federal government in Washington, also known as the American government: of the people, by the people, and for the people.

Like Reagan and Bush before him, Bill Clinton benefited from the general trend of good luck that characterized the years 1981 through 2000: no huge terrorist attacks, no unusual spate of natural disasters, and no mass baby boomer retirements. Thanks largely to internal problems in the Soviet Union, the United States avoided any prolonged military conflicts during this period. The only significant conflict was the 1991 Gulf War in Iraq, which, under Bush's leadership, was short and victorious. At the beginning of the twenty-year period, the markets corrected stagflation and revived the economy. At the end of the period, the dot-com boom would give the economy another boost. In between, George H. W. Bush would clean up the disaster of Reaganomics.

But in the 1990s, the nation hadn't yet overcome the myth that Reaganomics had somehow corrected the stagflation of the 1970s and early 1980s. Government regulations were viewed with suspicion even by some members of the Clinton administration, like Secretary of the Treasury Robert Rubin, a former Goldman Sachs chairman. In 1999, Bill Clinton signed legislation effectively repealing provisions of the 1933 Glass-Steagall Act, an important financial sector regulation that separated commercial banking and investment banking. This would have dire consequences in the next Republican administration where further resistance to regulation enabled the collapse of the home mortgage and securitization sector.

Despite his efforts to reduce regulation, Bill Clinton was faced with open hostility from congressional Republicans who eagerly exploited America's weak Constitution. They could make a mockery of the American government simply by refusing to act in good faith. Clinton cooperated with Republicans on welfare reform, the North American Free Trade Act, and a minimum wage increase. Like Bush, he raised taxes to keep the deficit in check. But after Clinton resisted reductions in Medicare, a critical Category I government function, Republicans shut down government twice, in 1995 and in 1996. The GOP's attack on the American government backfired when it helped Clinton get reelected in 1996.

Americans didn't realize it at the time, but they were witnessing the beginning of a new pattern in national politics. When in power, extremists in the Republican Party would exploit the misconception that Reaganomics had improved the economy in the 1980s; they would do everything possible to reduce government. When out of power, Republicans would disrupt the government with Senate filibusters, refusals to pay the nation's bills, and even government shutdowns. Either way, Republican resistance to the clear requirements of a modern economy worked to the detriment of the overwhelming majority of Americans.

Unfortunately, two decades of good luck would reinforce the myths about Reaganomics. How could attacking government possibly be wrong if the economy was so strong? But this era of relative peace and prosperity ended after 2000 when the nation got a taste of Reaganomics without Ronald Reagan's luck.

Chapter 9
Fool Me Twice: The Second Reagan Revolution: 2001–2008

Republican president George H. W. Bush was much reviled by many people in his own party as the man who pointed out the foolishness of Reaganomics. Reagan's "voodoo economics" would always fail for obvious reasons: government was necessary in a modern economy to make up for deficiencies in the markets, taxes provided almost all the revenue needed to pay for public sector activity, and regulations were essential to protect people from those in the private sector who would do them harm. Although there was considerable confusion among Americans about what ended stagflation in the 1980s, Reagan's huge budget deficits and the twin disasters of bankrupt S&Ls and the LBO turmoil on Wall Street provided empirical evidence of the failure of Reaganomics. The Reagan Revolution had apparently suffocated itself with unworkable policies; but after the 2000 presidential election, Reagan Republicans would try again.

Bush vs. Bush

As president, George H. W. Bush had stuck to his guns and corrected Reagan's mistakes, but the resulting lukewarm Republican support, independent presidential candidate Ross Perot, and a mild recession cost him reelection in 1992. George H. W. Bush effectively chose to be right rather than be president again.

In the 2000 election his eldest son, Republican presidential candidate George W. Bush, would have to make a choice: either follow in his father's footsteps and oppose Reaganomics, or cater to the Republican extremists and advocate nonsensical policies.

George W. Bush effectively chose to be wrong rather than not be president.

Shortly after taking office in 2001, George W. Bush mimicked Ronald Reagan's push for lower personal income taxes. There was justification for some of Reagan's tax cuts. In the 1980s, high oil prices caused rampant inflation, which prompted many employers to implement cost-of-living adjustments. This had pushed many lower- and middle-income Americans into unacceptably high tax brackets. But in 2001, there was no such excuse. The nation's economy would stabilize after the boom, bubble, and burst cycle of the dot-com era, so arbitrarily cutting taxes simply risked increasing the national debt. Americans had forgotten that inadequate tax revenue in the Reagan years had contributed to the largest peacetime budget deficits in American history.

So-called Reagan Republicans had promoted the idea that tax cuts would reduce federal government spending. But they didn't explain why it was desirable to do without necessities that weren't available from the private sector. In practice, Americans demanded these necessities even if it meant increased budget deficits.

George W. Bush's tax cuts didn't prevent the 9/11 terrorist attacks, the creation of the Department of Homeland Security, a massive expansion of the nation's intelligence capability, the wars in Afghanistan and Iraq, the retirement of millions of baby boomers, the Bush administration's twofold expansion of Medicare into Part D and Medicare Advantage Plans, and an unusual spate of natural disasters. Later, the Great Recession necessitated the TARP program, increases in food stamp distribution and unemployment compensation, and the 2009 stimulus plan.

Bush's ritualistic 2001 tax cuts were the beginning of the end of two hundred years of (relative) fiscal responsibility in the United

States. In *America's Fiscal Constitution*, Bill White's valuable history of federal budgeting, taxation, and debt, the corporate executive and former Houston mayor wrote: "The American fiscal tradition collapsed in 2001. Afterwards the federal government regularly borrowed a third or more of its expenses. Only part of the debt was used for the traditional purposes during war and a severe downturn. By 2014 federal debt had soared to almost $120,000 per working American."[50]

For a while, a bubble in the real estate markets and a wartime economy produced artificially high levels of economic activity that masked the ultimate futility of cutting taxes, increasing spending, and borrowing money to pay the bills. But by the beginning of his second term in 2005, George W. Bush had made a mockery of the first two principles of Reaganomics. He proved that government was frequently the solution to problems and that taxation was essential to minimizing the national debt. The third broken leg of the three-legged stool of Reaganomics would be the nation's economic undoing.

Inadequate Financial Regulation

The Reagan administration had clearly shown why inadequate regulation in the financial sector is a much greater threat to the nation than insufficient regulation in the real economy. Defects in baby cribs and automobiles, and improper ingredients in foods or drugs, get a lot of attention. But these problems are not likely to crash the stock market, cause mass unemployment, or force people from their homes. By contrast, people in the financial sector can quickly create billions of dollars of defective financial instruments—and set into motion the calamities previously mentioned—simply by typing on a computer keyboard.

Ronald Reagan's unfortunate deregulation of the savings and

loan industry had allowed and encouraged the foolish commercial lending that precipitated the S&L crisis (chapter 7). But more important for future reference was the leveraged buyouts, greenmail, insider trading, and junk bond turmoil on Wall Street that seemed to spring forth automatically in response to Reagan's antiregulatory beliefs. Those fiascos revealed the danger of a federal government run by people naive enough to believe that markets alone would protect the American people from internal defects in markets.

From the beginning of the George W. Bush administration, there was a perfect storm of gullibility, with the White House and both houses of Congress run by antiregulatory zealots. As in the 1980s, Wall Street leaped at the opportunity. But what area of the economy should they exploit? By 2002, the single-most-conspicuous feature of the financial sector was the low interest rates created by Federal Reserve chairman Alan Greenspan. These were intended to spur economic activity after the end of the dot-com boom and following the 9/11 terrorist attacks. But Wall Street saw low interest rates as an opportunity to inject itself into two of the most conservative areas of finance, home mortgage lending and mortgage securitization.

Long-term lending is inherently risky. Over a period of many years, just about anything could go wrong in a borrower's life. Historically, mortgage lenders protected themselves from this risk by accepting only loans that met high standards. But in the early twenty-first century, Wall Street would change all that. Shortly after the dust settled on 9/11, bankers rushed into mortgage securitization. Every American should ponder why, in a very short period of time, an industry that had always done everything right because it had to, started doing everything wrong because it could get away with it.

People in the financial sector don't want to do a deal and make a million dollars. They want to do a thousand deals and make a billion dollars. So the bankers who entered mortgage securitization needed more mortgages, the raw material of mortgage securities. The word quickly went out to mortgage lenders that high lending standards were a thing of the past. "Send us your tired, your poor, your subprime, your absurd mortgages." A real estate bubble swept the nation as even unqualified borrowers in some areas found that they could easily get loans for overpriced houses. No-down-payment, adjustable-rate mortgage loans became increasingly common. A market unfettered by government regulation flexed its powerful muscles.

The Great Recession

The irresponsible lending scheme inevitably failed, and by the end of 2007, the Great Recession had begun. Millions of Americans lost their homes, jobs, savings, and good credit ratings as the country descended into the worst economic downturn since the Great Depression. The stock market collapsed and many financial firms were at risk of default. As so frequently happens in a market economy, government provided the only viable solutions to a huge problem. In 2008, the Bush administration convinced a Democratically controlled Congress to support the TARP program, a government bailout of the financial sector. It would take years to unwind the damage done to the nation's economy. Some Americans would never fully recover.[*]

Why was the disaster of inadequate regulation under George W. Bush so much worse than the twin disasters of the S&L crisis and the LBO fiasco in the Reagan administration? In the 1980s,

---

[*]   The Great Recession is described in more detail in my other book, *America in the Economic World: Jobs, Necessities, and Economic Optimization* (Minneapolis: Langdon Street Press, 2014), 151–67.

the S&L crisis and the LBO fiasco were mainly limited to business-to-business transactions. S&Ls made foolish loans to commercial developers. Corporate raiders went after vulnerable businesses. Managers profited by taking their own companies private. Ordinary Americans weren't directly affected. But during the Bush administration, many Americans were hurt in the worst possible ways: they lost homes, savings, and jobs.

The Great Recession didn't have to happen. The Bush administration ignored repeated warnings from many prominent experts that irresponsible lending would inevitably crash the mortgage markets and bring down the financial sector. Those who offered warnings included Nobel Prize–winning economist Joseph Stiglitz, New York University economist Nouriel Roubini, financier George Soros, Morgan Stanley's Stephen Roach, Yale University housing expert Robert Shiller, and former Council of Economic Advisors member Robert Westcott.[51]

Unfortunately, the quasi-religious nature of antigovernment ideology prevented any regulatory intervention. Instead, the American people would get the TARP program and the 2009 stimulus plan, two Category I functions of government. Also, expansions of two Category IV government functions, food stamps and unemployment compensation, were necessary to alleviate widespread misery. Just as in the Reagan years, neglecting a critical Category II government function (financial regulation) necessitated a public sector remedy to big private sector market problems.

The Aftermath

Recessions are defined by declining national output. But economists recognize that unemployment is a lagging indicator of an economic downturn, i.e. job losses would continue even after the official end of the Great Recession on June 30,

2009. Unemployment would grow to just above 10 percent. This was almost as high as the 10.8 percent rate in the Reagan administration, a post–Great Depression record. A big decline in all forms of taxable income (personal, corporate, and investment income), combined with increased government spending and Bush's tax cuts, guaranteed massive budget deficits for years to come. The national debt would soar to more than $18 trillion.

The world breathed a sigh of relief when George W. Bush left the White House in January 2009. Bush had become the poster child for Reaganomics. His foreign policy (more details to come in chapter 10) had also offended many people. Bush was succeeded by Democrat Barack Obama, a former Illinois senator. Obama was immediately awarded the Nobel Peace Prize—for not being George W. Bush.

Barack Obama was elected by the American people to perform three critical missions: ease the pain of the Great Recession, implement policies that would prevent another economic disaster, and get the United States out of the second Iraq War. Obama's economic role would be similar to that of Republican president George H. W. Bush in 1989, who was expected to clean up the mess created by Reagan's eight years in office.

The big question was whether or not Republicans would allow Obama to straighten out a Republican-created economic disaster. Twenty years earlier, extremists in the GOP had clashed with Republican president George H. W. Bush when he raised taxes to reduce Reagan's huge budget deficits. By 2009, however, Republican moderates were so scarce that it would be impossible for Congress to muster a bipartisan effort to correct the nation's economic problems. Budget deficits and unemployment would flow from the George W. Bush recession for years.

Antigovernment zealots had taken over the party of Lincoln,

Teddy Roosevelt, and Eisenhower. They criticized and even punished Republicans who acted in good faith to make government work. Republicans who wanted to keep their seats in Congress had to toe the party line or be faced with a well-funded opponent in their next GOP primary. The world hadn't witnessed such a mindless commitment to ideology since the heyday of Communism in the Soviet Union.

The Obama administration managed to pass an $800 billion stimulus package in 2009. This wasn't a lot of money given the magnitude of the Great Recession, but Obama's stimulus would ultimately be credited with placing a floor on the economic downturn. Republicans ridiculed the stimulus as just more big government.

Republicans also opposed the 2011 creation of the Consumer Financial Protection Bureau, an agency charged with preventing the mistakes in the financial sector that had caused the Great Recession. The fact that the economic disaster was made possible by inadequate regulation; i.e., too little government, didn't alter either the pervasive ideological impairment or the desire for political advantage in the Republican Party. However, despite Republican resistance, the CFPB would quickly prove to be effective at helping ordinary Americans deal with unfair practices in the financial sector.

Cautionary Tales

By the time George W. Bush took office, Reaganomics had infected all aspects of government. At the national, state, and local levels, the proper economic role of public policy is to make up for the inadequacies of private sector markets. The defining characteristic of a modern economy is that, for practical purposes, people do not produce any of the necessities of life for themselves. Their survival requires that the surrounding economic system works, and government is inescapably part of that system. It is therefore not surprising that attempts to use Reaganomics to thwart proper state government policies have also failed miserably. Some examples will illustrate the problems:

- Kansas

    Reagan Republicans took over state government in Kansas in 2011 and followed what is by now a familiar formula: they cut taxes and reduced government spending, depriving some people of necessities that they couldn't get from the private sector. When the tax cuts predictably caused big state budget shortfalls, the same politicians claimed that government was too big and so, clearly, the state budget needed to be slashed even further. Education was particularly hard-hit. The length of the school year was reduced, classrooms were closed, teachers were fired, and local property taxes were increased.[52]

    Wealthy donors from other states sent campaign contributions to Kansas politicians who supported anti-government policies and changes in tax laws that further shifted the burden of taxation to poor people. Now, the lowest-earning quintile in Kansas pays an average of 11.1 percent of what they make in state and local taxes. The wealthiest 1 percent, by contrast, pays an average of just 3.6 percent of their annual income.[53]

    Naturally, Kansas opted out of the extra federal Medicaid funding provided by President Obama's Affordable Care Act. These funds were designed to help poor people get adequate health care. Today, at both the state and national level, the part of the population burdened by inadequate employment, unemployment, and just plain bad luck suffers the most from attempts to avoid modern economic reality. But Kansas has been particularly hard-hit as increased budget deficits cause more and more reductions in spending. The newest threats are to public pensions and highways.[54] Too many people have forgotten that the five categories of government functions described in chapter 1 exist for good reasons.

"Toto, I don't think we're in America anymore. We're in Kansas!"

• Louisiana

In 2008, the Bayou State was still recovering from the double disasters of Hurricane Katrina and the Bush Recession when it added ideological impairment to its litany of woes. Reagan Republicans were elected to run a state government blessed with a $1 billion surplus thanks to high oil prices and federal disaster relief funds. But Republicans followed the usual formula and enacted the largest tax cut in state history. This, together with a downturn in the historically wobbly oil industry, quickly created a $1.6 billion deficit that "necessitated" state budget cuts.

Once again, the pattern in antigovernment tactics was clear. When times are good, pretend that they will be good forever, and cut taxes. When the economy cycles down (and it always will eventually), shrink government to accommodate the predictable decline in tax revenue. Then, blame the usual culprits (the poor, the elderly, the sick, the unemployed, retirees, students, and government employees) for their inability to use the private sector alone to solve all their problems.

In recent years, laid-off state employees have joined unemployed oil field workers in seeking government benefits. A rational tax and budget policy would have maintained public employment as an economic stabilizer. As it is, increased unemployment is not likely to turn the Louisiana economy around anytime soon. Perversely, Louisiana maintained taxpayer subsidies for private sector, for-profit television and movie productions in the state.[55]

As in Kansas, budget cuts were disproportionately directed at education. But in Louisiana, the target was mainly state colleges and universities. Education is an important Category III function of government. It is the key ingredient in achieving economic success for most people, states, and nations. Historically, government has provided or subsidized everything from kindergarten to graduate school. These subsidies are necessary because of well-known inadequacies in the private sector markets, especially inadequate employment, that prevent most people from simply buying an education. Nationally, there has been a widespread effort by antigovernment market purists to reduce public funding for higher education with the goal of "letting the market handle it." But for most Americans, that is an economic and mathematical impossibility.

Between 2008 and 2014, Louisiana reduced per-student funding for higher education by 43 percent. Louisiana State University had to let go of nearly two thousand employees, including about 360 faculty members. All other public colleges were similarly affected. This is devastating to a state that has the country's highest rate of young adults neither working nor in school. In addition, Louisiana is next to last in the nation in college attainment, with just 29 percent of adults possessing a college degree.[56] This assault on higher education will benefit Louisiana politicians if an uneducated electorate is less resistant to bad public policy.

- Texas

Since the 1901 discovery of the big Spindletop oil field in southeast Texas, the state has benefited from huge amounts of oil and natural gas revenue. To fully understand the peculiarities of the Texas economy, one must compare it to other petro states (those with an economy dominated by hydrocarbon production). Here we use the word "state" in the most general sense to indicate a well-defined territory with its own government.

Alaska, another petro state, has larger per-capita revenue from the oil industry than Texas, but its proximity to the North Pole limits business investment. As a result, Alaska redistributes its oil revenue to state residents who can put it to good use for warm clothing, food, rifles, pickup trucks, and assorted wilderness equipment.

Like Alaska, the petro state of Saudi Arabia suffers from a harsh climate that limits non-oil and natural gas investments within the country. The Saudis use their hydrocarbon income to fund the national budget, the Saudi royal family, and a large sovereign wealth fund that can invest anywhere in the world. Their income from oil revenues was about $300 billion in 2012.[57]

By contrast, Texas has a more favorable climate than either Alaska or Saudi Arabia. So Texans can put oil revenue to good use in infrastructure, education, banking, retailing, and numerous other investments. The abundance of oil and natural gas beneath the ground has produced many cumulative benefits since 1901 and spared Texas dependence on cattle, cotton, corn, soybeans, and other agricultural products. Even a century of ideal weather wouldn't have allowed the level of prosperity from agriculture that the state has received from oil and gas.

In the 1990s, Reagan Republicans stepped into this happy situation and—well, by now you know the drill. Tax cuts and resistance to public sector spending soon followed. For a while, high oil prices and increased shale fracking created a boom that temporarily masked much of the damage. But a worldwide decline in oil prices in 2014 (see chapter 6) brought the state back down to earth.

Even when times were good, the state didn't address

chronic problems such as poverty and huge numbers of citizens without health insurance. These will surely be ignored as the state's oil industry suffers one of its frequent downturns. Of course, Texas opted out of extra Medicaid funding provided by the Affordable Care Act. This money would have violated widespread anti–federal government sentiment. But that decision will cost the state about $90 billion in federal funds over ten years and will force Texans to pay for indigent medical care with local tax revenue.

Reagan Republicans ended the long-standing practice of pay-as-you-go spending on transportation infrastructure at the same time that prosperity placed a strain on highways all over the state. In the booming Eagle Ford Shale fracking area, paved roads were torn up by lucrative private sector economic activity. So formerly paved roads were replaced by gravel roads. Funding shifted to bonds and toll roads, and as a result, state bond indebtedness rose considerably. This mimicked the rise in the national debt after the applications of Reaganomics under both Ronald Reagan and George W. Bush.

Texas's peculiar success cannot be exported to other states. It is not possible to economically inject large quantities of oil and natural gas into the ground so that they can then be "discovered" and produce economic prosperity. The Texas model looks good only if one is willing to overlook the neglect of millions of its citizens. But the model works for antigovernment politicians. High oil prices can cover up the failure of Reaganomics by providing the illusions of a successful economy and good public policy. At other times, low oil prices can be blamed for the state's economic problems.

In Kansas, Louisiana, and Texas, Reaganomics maintains its perfect track record: it fails at every level of government. But couldn't that cause problems for the GOP at election time?

Republicans had two main concerns after the 2008 election of Democrat Barack Obama. First, they needed to make the Obama administration look bad. After eight years of continuous disasters, the Democrats were bound to be seen as an improvement. Second, they needed to salvage George W. Bush's reputation. Reaganomics had been the backbone of his domestic policies, but if voters ever put two and two together, they would realize that these policies defied everything they had known all their lives. Government was an important part of the economy without which markets couldn't work properly.

Paradoxically, these political problems would be addressed by using Reaganomics again, but this time as a political strategy. While it always fails as an economic policy, the mythology of Reaganomics works as a political tactic at both the state and national levels. Distractions and inflammatory speech can be combined to take advantage of the natural antigovernment bias mentioned in chapter 2. Reagan himself had demonstrated that voters readily fell for "feel-good" platitudes, antigovernment jokes, and appeals to turn against Washington in the name of freedom. This magnifies existing antigovernment bias and causes Americans to increasingly question the competence of the people who are ultimately responsible for their government—namely, themselves. Reaganomics as a political strategy will be the subject of part III.

Part III

Reaganomics as Political Strategy

Chapter 10
From Jokes and Distractions to Government Shutdowns and War

Reaganomics' dismal record begs the question: How does a political minority that has been out of step with the needs of the American people since the 1930s get elected to high office despite advocating economic policies that have always failed, policies that attempt to thwart the well-defined requirements of a modern economy? The only answer is that Reaganomics is an effective political strategy posing as an economic theory.

In 2013, a group of self-proclaimed Reagan Republicans shut down the federal government and inflicted grave harm to the nation's economy, which lost $24 billion in economic activity in two days. These elected officials readily admitted that the sole purpose of the shutdown was to cater to their political base. There was no pretense that the attack would serve any useful public purpose; it was simply an antigovernment political tactic designed to get people reelected.

Reaganomics has dominated public discourse in America since 1980. In some political circles, it is axiomatic that the American government must be attacked, shrunk, underfunded, ridiculed, impeded, and even closed down. This undermines the US Constitution and violates the clear requirements of a modern economy (chapter 1). The damage done by Reaganomics as an economic policy (chapters 7–9) is often the consequence of sedition masquerading as free market advocacy.

The translation of Reaganomics from economic theory to political strategy is straightforward:

- Government is not the solution; government is the problem.
  Politicians can easily take advantage of natural antigovernment bias by appealing to voters' distrust of government. "You hate government. I hate government. Vote for me and I'll go to Washington (or the state capital) and destroy government on your behalf."
- Cut taxes.
  "Vote for me and I'll cut your taxes. Since you'll have more money after the tax reduction, I'm going to pay you to vote for me."
- Reduce regulations.
  Corporations and wealthy businesspeople are the best sources of funds for political campaigns. "Send my campaign money, and after I'm elected, I will not regulate your business. You can do to the American people as you damn well please."

It is easy to get votes for failed economic theories if people want to believe in them. But politicians using this political strategy are taking a big chance: voters might remember that in our modern economy, people rely for their very survival on the fact that Reaganomics is utter nonsense. Government is often the solution to critical problems (defense, disaster relief, education, police protection, Medicare, etc.), taxes pay the government's bills, and regulations protect ordinary people from those who would do them harm. So antigovernment politicians must be prepared to divert people's attention away from economic reality and toward irrelevant or imagined issues.

We can divide the numerous distractions used to divert the public's attention into two categories. First are excuses that try to explain away the repeated failure of antigovernment policy. We label this category "Apologetics." The second category, "Hysterics," consists of emotional and inflammatory statements that effectively give people something to gripe about so they won't pay attention to things that matter. Political operatives may offer these two diversions at the same time.

Apologetics

Since Reaganomics always fails as economic policy, it's essential that politicians using it as a political strategy have at their disposal a ready arsenal of statements to deflect the public's attention. By now, most Americans are familiar with this assault on public discourse.

A good example of using distractions to divert the public's attention occurred during the George W. Bush administration after inadequate regulation enabled the Great Recession. Politicians and economists who had advocated mortgage lending and mortgage securitization unfettered by regulations were humiliated. They had repeated one of Reagan's mistakes, but this time the consequences were much worse. Americans were losing their homes, their jobs, and their savings.

These market purists needed to get ahead of public opinion before people realized that internal defects in the financial markets had caused another problem. So they resorted to the same tactic that had worked so well for Reagan: blame Jimmy Carter for everything. They claimed that the Community Redevelopment Act of 1977, a "Jimmy Carter–era law," had caused the massive economic downturn.

The CRA excuse was widely disseminated by party operatives and compliant media. It became the weapon of choice in a desperate, and largely successful, effort to salvage Reaganomics. In addition to knowing what actually caused the problem (see

chapter 9), we know at least six reasons that the CRA did not cause
the problem:

- The CRA was designed to encourage mortgage lending.
  But one of the causes of the Great Recession was that it
  was *too easy* to get mortgage loans.

- The CRA was a regulation. But another cause of the Great
  Recession was that the Bush administration was not
  inclined to support regulations.

- From 2002 to 2007, most of the problem mortgage
  lending was for home purchases by middle- and upper-
  income buyers. But the CRA was mainly created to help
  people in poor neighborhoods get loans.

- It was not necessary to go back thirty years to Jimmy
  Carter to find a president who was pushing home ownership. The George W. Bush administration's domestic
  policy, the Ownership Society, was contemporaneously
  encouraging people to buy homes. But his administration was so busy making so many mistakes on such a
  massive scale (the second Iraq War, neglecting Hurricane Katrina victims, arbitrarily cutting taxes, unfunded
  expansions of Medicare, inadequate financial regulations, etc.) that Bush's domestic program never became
  well-known.

- The Texas bankers who run the Dallas Federal Reserve
  Bank did a formal research study to determine the
  impact of the CRA on the economic downturn. These
  bankers are typically conservative Republicans. In 2009,
  they released their results, which concluded that the CRA
  did not cause the Great Recession. That made it official.[58]

- Since 2009, there have been numerous multibillion-dollar
  civil suits brought against the financial sector by all the

attorneys general of every state along with the federal attorney general. The plaintiffs have almost always won, often getting huge judgments against financial firms that caused the Great Recession. At no time during this still-ongoing legal process has anyone ever invoked the CRA as an excuse for their actions.

Among the other reasons offered as a cause of the Great Recession was the notion that Fannie Mae, "a quasi-government agency," was the culprit. But in the big civil lawsuits mentioned above, Fannie Mae was a plaintiff, not a defendant. More comically, it was suggested that Bush's successor, Democratic president Barack Obama, caused the Great Recession. But Obama didn't take office until about a year and a half after the downturn started.

Pro-Reaganomics politicians tried to explain away the huge budget deficits and massive increases in the national debt following Bush's recession by claiming that these were the fault of "big government programs" started by previous Democratic administrations. But the United States was in good financial shape when George W. Bush took office in early 2001 following the dot-com boom. Bush's predecessor, Democrat Bill Clinton, had a budget surplus. Simple arithmetic suggests that subsequent deficits resulted from a combination of irresponsible tax cuts and big spending increases in the Bush administration.

Antitax policies are easily exploited by political operatives. But Bush inadvertently refuted two claims that have often been useful vote-getters. His administration proved that tax cuts cannot reduce federal government spending (see chapter 9). Also, tax cuts are not an effective economic stimulus since they require borrowing money to make up for lost revenue. Under the most optimistic assumptions for both a multiplier effect and for recaptured tax revenue after the "stimulus", a federal income tax cut will simply increase the national debt. An exception occurs only when there is a combination of income growth and sufficiently high marginal tax rates (after the tax cut), like the nation experienced in the Johnson administration in the 1960s.

Oftentimes, there is an appeal to "freedom" as a rationale for economic policies that have undermined the role of government in a modern economy: In lieu of paying taxes, Americans should be "free" to borrow money from China to pay for government services. Business regulations that address internal market defects (Category II government functions) are impediments to the freedom of businessmen. Our needs should come from the free market economy. These calls for freedom invariably strike an emotional chord in voters.

But without government to compensate for the inadequacies of the marketplace, personal economic viability itself may be jeopardized. Without economic viability there is no life. And without life, there is neither liberty nor the pursuit of happiness.

Americans who lost their homes and savings due to lack of financial regulations, who are concerned about the impact on future generations of excessive tax cuts and the huge national debt, who must go deeply into debt themselves in order to go to college, or who fear that their health insurance will be taken away by extremist politicians, find little consolation in the abstract notion that they have more personal "freedom."

Hysterics

If "reasoning" doesn't work, then nonsense can be just as useful. No one was more effective at ridiculing serious discussion of the federal government's proper economic functions than Ronald Reagan. Indeed, his January 1981 comment that government wasn't the solution, it was the problem, was probably a little joke that got out of hand. Thanks to Reagan's followers, this false and inflammatory remark became the most destructive statement in American history.

Each year since 1980, inflammatory speech has been increasingly effective in diverting the public's attention. Americans are encouraged to make jokes about serious things. At the same time, they are told to take nonsense seriously.

Illegal voters are all over the place, undermining elections and threatening the republic! But nobody can find them. Nevertheless, this myth has been wielded as a tool to restrict voting by minorities, students, senior citizens, people with health problems, and the poor.

Illegal immigrants are overrunning the nation! The American people, almost all of whom are the descendants of immigrants, are allegedly fed up with it. Especially repugnant are dastardly people migrating to America to better support their families, and children coming from Central America to escape pervasive violence in their home countries. A Congress rendered dysfunctional by politicians pushing a failed economic theory cannot rationally address this bipartisan issue (conservative businessmen appreciate the cheap labor, liberals see immigrants as future voters, many conservatives want to secure the borders, and labor unions do not want an influx of workers willing to accept low wages).

President Barack Obama is not a legal citizen of the United States! Moreover, he is secretly a Muslim. Like the notion that the "Jimmy Carter–era law" caused the Great Recession, many Americans cannot seem to get this nonsense out of their minds; "out of their minds" being the operative phrase. The so-called "birther" issue became the litmus test for political gullibility.

Since government is evil, the lingering effects of the global recession that began in 2007 require tax cuts and higher interest rates (both of which favor wealthy people). Also, we should shrink government spending even though it provides both necessities and jobs that will not come from the private sector. These policies are collectively called austerity. But the United States has had a relatively strong recovery from the Great Recession largely because, unlike Europe, it avoided austerity.

Government spending, slight tax increases, Barack Obama's 2009 stimulus, and the Federal Reserve System's quantitative easing policies have combined with the inherent strengths in America's economic system to produce a fairly strong recovery since the end of the Bush administration. Actually, "unfairly strong recovery" might be a better description. As we'll see in chapter 13, many people increasingly suffer from inadequate employment, which, by definition, describes jobs that prevent workers from providing themselves with all the necessities of life.

People who favor big government want to burden the United States with "European socialism." The proper economic role of government is to help Americans overcome inadequacies in the private sector marketplace. The use of government in this regard is a nonideological response to real problems. But it is hard for people whose heads are filled with Reaganomics to accept the pragmatic reasons why national defense, Medicare, public education, infrastructure, law enforcement, financial sector regulation, antiterrorist activity, the courts and prison system, health regulations, disaster relief, Social Security, and many other economic functions must flow through government in a modern economy.

There is no lower limit to the nonsensical notions that are used to divert people's attention from bad economic policies. Some, such as the repeated claim that former vice president Al Gore said he invented the Internet, are benign and even comical. However, other distractions are stark reminders of the sordid history of the anti-American government movement.

The massive shift of Southern white segregationists from the Democratic Party in the 1960s and 1970s made the GOP the default home for racists who wanted to align themselves with a major political party. The "solid South" has become a very reliable voting bloc for Republicans. This explains why Ronald Reagan began his 1980 presidential campaign in Mississippi. After Democrats helped elect America's first black president in 2008, racist political cartoons and comments began to appear in any media that would accept them.

Nationally, subtle prejudices can yield more votes than overt racism. It's easy to divide and conquer voters simply by getting people riled up. In a large, diverse nation, emotional fault lines can be created everywhere: taxpayers vs. welfare mothers, businessmen who oppose environmentalists and regulators, people in poor neighborhoods in conflict with law enforcement, evangelical conservatives who proclaim that gay marriage is against their religious beliefs, gun owners insisting on their right to bear arms everywhere, and after 9/11, many Americans who express hostility toward Muslims. An angry voter is not likely to spend much time thinking about disastrous economic policies that will likely cause him more harm than all the emotional issues combined.

Fear of Big Bird

In 2012, many Americans were stunned when Republican presidential candidate Mitt Romney declared that if elected, he would eliminate public funding for PBS. The press called it a threat to Big Bird, the giant yellow character on PBS's *Sesame Street*. PBS funding is a Category V government function motivated by the public's desire for noncommercial broadcasting.

For years, polls have regularly indicated that Americans

consider PBS to be among the nation's most trusted institutions.[59] But Romney had to cater to the "Republican base," the far-right-wing element of the party that traces its origins back to Goldwater's supporters in the 1960s. Despite public broadcasting's track record of showing both sides of critical issues, these voters claimed that there was a liberal bias in the media. Perhaps "showing both sides of critical issues" was the problem.

In fact, during the George W. Bush administration, PBS was criticized for exhibiting a conservative bias because it sometimes showed the 2003 Iraq War in a favorable light. The liberal media referred to the PBS documentary *America at a Crossroads* as "a neoconservative propaganda series."[60] Good journalism is bound to rile up everybody at least some of the time.

The nation's support for PBS speaks for itself. Most people recognized that the attack on Big Bird was just political posturing by antigovernment extremists who had already done considerable damage to the country. Gerrymandered congressional districts, Senate filibusters, government shutdowns, refusal to legislate in good faith, and impediments to legal voting were a far greater threat to the United States than using a little of the taxpayers' money to partly fund PBS.

The Big Noise

In politics, the best defense is often a good offense. With the airwaves and print media currently saturated with nonsense, busy voters don't have enough time to sort out fact from fiction. This lack of attention means lies gain traction and never lose it (e.g., the CRA, Fannie Mae, and Barack Obama caused the Great Recession).

At one time, political parties had to pay for campaign litera-ture mailings, phone banks, and most media exposure. Talk wasn't cheap. But the development of the Internet and social media has made it possible to contact millions of voters regularly at almost no cost. Public opinion can be massaged gradually by flooding the World Wide Web with unflattering photos and inflammatory articles about elected officials. In addition, an in-house broadcasting network can even offer biased programming sponsored by commercial advertisers.

The Supreme Court's *Citizens United* ruling allows corporations to inject virtually unlimited amounts of money into promoting nominally political views. America's founding fathers would be appalled that the government they created unduly favors corporations, nonhuman entities whose owners (shareholders) may well have opinions not reflected by the company's management. Would a pro-life shareholder approve of support for a pro-choice official just because the official opposes government regulation of certain corporate activities? Shouldn't a business simply make its case in the proper public forum rather than injecting shareholders' money into the political process?

The saddest political tactic has been the practice of using continuous ridicule and humor to reduce government and democracy to jokes. Ronald Reagan excelled at this. Example: "A taxpayer is someone who works for the federal government but doesn't have to take a civil service exam."[61]

Ironically, it is the persistent failure of Reaganomics as economic policy that has increased the public's skepticism about government, reinforced natural antigovernment bias, and made a mockery of public discourse. The notion that the country "survived" Jimmy Carter still gets laughs in certain political circles. This despite the fact that only lucky market timing saved Reagan. After that, Reaganomics itself became a greater disaster for the nation than stagflation; witness the Great Recession. Most of America's current economic problems stem from the fact that the nation did not survive Ronald Reagan.

Once the most reliable supporters of sound fiscal policy, conservatives found that tax cuts could be an effective weapon against the federal government. These individuals could be rewarded with tax breaks and a chance to blame the resulting budget deficits on "big government." Meanwhile, constant government bashing has created paranoia in certain gullible populations. In 2015, a routine US Army exercise in central Texas alarmed the natives, who feared a federal government takeover. The Texas governor sent in the Texas State Guard to "monitor" the federal troops.[62] A historically pro-military population now distrusts our men and women in uniform. Obviously, the nation has paid a heavy price for decades of anti-American government political propaganda.

Devolution

The never-ending flow of distractions, noise, and nonsense to prop up failed public policies has produced many casualties. One casualty that cannot be measured in dollars and cents is the loss of the concept of "fact." People seem more eager than ever to accept demonstrable falsehoods. Even worse, they will not change their minds when presented with the truth.

Academic studies at numerous institutions have shown that when misinformed people are exposed to facts, they rarely change their minds. Insecure people are especially reluctant to alter their opinions, and thus become the easy prey of demagogues. They live in constant fear of illegal voters, the US Army, European socialism, Big Bird, and a Muslim president. Educated and sophisticated people may or may not be insecure, but they are even more resistant to changing their minds. After all, they're used to being right most of the time. This is particularly disastrous since, according to political scientist Larry M. Bartels, "The political ignorance of the American voter is one of the best-documented data in political science."[63]

By the twenty-first century, tactics that began with Ronald Reagan's good-natured jokes had descended into a brutal mockery of the American government in Washington. No lie was too outrageous if it got votes. Public discourse and the media were filled with so much nonsense that an actual deterioration in the ability of many voters to think properly became evident. The Republican base bore the brunt of this assault on the intellect, but the entire nation suffered. It wasn't clear whether America's weak Constitution, which required elected officials to act in good faith if government was to work properly, could stand up to this rapid decline in the quality of the American electorate and its choices at the polls.

For many Americans, especially those who lost jobs to technology and the global economy, the world has become a scary place. These unlucky citizens have become perfect prey for those seeking political advantage by claiming that the government of the people, by the people, and for the people, is out to get them. The business world compounds the problem by offering massive compensation to an elite group of managers and highly skilled professionals while many jobs that once supported a family now pay very little or have disappeared altogether. Workers with the same expectations as their parents cannot understand why their 1950s-style educations, skills, and work ethics don't translate into middle-class prosperity. Moreover, the country is no longer made up of the comfortably homogeneous population that many Americans remember from their childhood.

"Making" War

The distractions described in this chapter have been painfully effective at undermining good public policy. As a result, Americans have suffered from inadequate financial regulation, the S&L crisis, the leveraged buyout fiasco, the Great Recession, a dysfunctional Congress, huge budget deficits, and a dramatic increase in the national debt. Without Reaganomics, these events either would have not occurred at all or would have been much less severe.

Unfortunately, the same political techniques used to get anti-government officials elected were also effective in promoting the second Iraq War. Americans were overwhelmed with propaganda prior to the 2003 war in Iraq. Critics were ridiculed as cowards, soft on terrorism, unpatriotic, or worse. Public debate was tainted by misinformation. Reporters who criticized the war were threatened with lack of access to the White House.

The 1991 Gulf War in Iraq had been a surgically precise operation, at least compared with military actions that preceded and followed it. Under the leadership of President George H. W. Bush, the United States put together a coalition of nations to repel Saddam Hussein's invasion of Kuwait while protecting nearby Saudi Arabia. This provided security for two of the world's most important oil-exporting countries. The Gulf Coalition greatly punished Hussein's military and damaged Iraqi infrastructure.

After the 1991 war, the UN's oil-for-food program kept Iraq from using export revenue to replace damaged military equipment. In addition, the United States instituted the Policy of Containment in which American fighter jets overflew Iraq 24/7. Any structure in Iraq could be taken out on short notice with little danger to any American. Saddam would have been foolish to use weapons of mass destruction, if he had any. Though still an enemy state, Iraq was no longer a threat to either its neighbors or the United States.

Suspicious Minds

Nevertheless, in 2002 and 2003 Americans were assured that Iraq was developing weapons of mass destruction and/or had somehow participated with al-Qaeda in the 9/11 terrorist attacks. This received wisdom was effectively rammed down the throats of the American public with the same techniques that for decades had promoted failed economic theories. Coercion and ridicule were used to intimidate any journalist or elected official who dared suggest that the George W. Bush administration was too hasty in its eagerness to add another battlefront. These were the same tactics that had been used since the 1980s by extremists in the Republican Party to fend off criticism of Reaganomics.

The Bush administration tossed around numerous justifications for going to war, apparently trying to make something stick. The entire exercise seemed contrived, especially the suggestions that Saddam Hussein was part of the 9/11 plot or that he had allowed an al-Qaeda training camp on Iraqi soil. A connection to al-Qaeda was illogical since Hussein was notorious for his refusal to ally himself with anybody, let alone a whole terrorist network.

So the default reason for attacking Iraq was the claim that it had weapons of mass destruction (WMDs). Had Saddam retained stockpiles of the chemical weapons that he had used in the 1980s? The Bush administration seemed to insinuate that Iraq had developed new weapons. But neither American intelligence, British intelligence, nor United Nations inspectors had turned up any evidence of WMDs.

Ultimately, the George W. Bush administration fell back on the same argument that had been used for years to justify Reaganomics: they were right and anybody who disagreed with them was wrong. By late 2002, the Bush administration had declared its firm intention to invade Iraq, go to Baghdad, and overthrow Saddam Hussein.

As secretary of defense in the George H. W. Bush administration, George W. Bush's vice president, Dick Cheney, had supported the decision not to go to Baghdad in 1991. In a 1994 interview at the American Enterprise Institute, Cheney gave a long list of reasons why an invasion of Baghdad would have been foolish:[64]

- There would be no Arab support for the war.
- The war would effectively be an American invasion.
- The United States would create instability that might cause Iraqi Kurds to join Turkish Kurds in a war against Turkey.
- Syria might claim western Iraq.
- Iran, already the most dangerous country in the Middle East, might seize eastern Iraq.
- There was no viable substitute for Saddam Hussein's government.
- Going to Baghdad was not worth the large sacrifice of American lives.

All of Cheney's reasons for not invading Baghdad in 1991 still applied at the start of the 2003 Iraq War. Yet the expressed intention of the United States in 2003 was to go to Baghdad and overthrow Saddam Hussein. What could possibly have precipitated an action that Vice President Dick Cheney had previously claimed made no sense?

The evidence of weapons of mass destruction in Iraq was so weak that the decision to go back to war in 2003 begs another explanation. Could there have been another reason to put tens of thousands of Americans in harm's way in Iraq again? Four other possibilities exist, but three of these can probably be dismissed out of hand.

Could Bush have been trying to appease his Evangelical Christian supporters by destroying what some of them considered to be the Great Satan in the Middle East, Saddam Hussein? Was Bush retaliating for Hussein's alleged threats against his father, George H. W. Bush, after the 1991 war? These were very flimsy reasons to send a nation to war.

Perhaps there was a third reason: George W. Bush wanted to enhance his status as a wartime president prior to the 2004 presidential election. By 2003, the war in Afghanistan was already seen as fairly nebulous. Domestically, the war on terrorism consisted largely of inconvenient security checks at airports, throwing federal money indiscriminately at local police departments, and a massive and hugely expensive expansion of the nation's intelligence operations. But going out on a limb to create a pretext for another war in Iraq solely for political advantage was risky. Maybe there was a better reason.

Peak Oil

By 2014, dramatic increases in US oil production from shale fracking and Gulf of Mexico drilling had fundamentally changed the global oil markets (see chapter 6). The world seemed to be awash in oil, and as a result, oil prices collapsed. But this wasn't always the case. We need to go back to the 1991 Gulf War to understand why concern about secure sources of energy might have led to the 2003 invasion of Iraq.

During and after the 1991 Iraq War, Republican president George H. W. Bush was severely criticized by members of his own party for not invading Baghdad and overthrowing Saddam Hussein. It wasn't unusual for the right wing of the Republican Party to attack Bush's policies (chapter 8). After all, he was a member of the wrong wing of the GOP, later dubbed the "Establishment Republicans." But numerous politicians, people in the oil industry, and many earth scientists around the world knew of an impending world economic crisis: the strong possibility of a global oil shortage.

For many years, geologists had observed that newly discovered oil fields contained fewer and fewer reserves than those found in the past. There is a simple but reasonable explanation for this: it is easier to hit a big target than a small target. So, big oil fields tended to be discovered first. Moreover, big fields are far more profitable. The concern about the preponderance of smaller discoveries gave rise to the notion of "peak oil"; i.e., world oil production would soon reach some maximum level and then decline.

A reduced energy supply combined with a rapidly expanding global economy would spell disaster. New countries were entering world markets and some of them, like China and India, had huge populations. They threatened to put hundreds of millions of new vehicles on the road. The stagflation created by the OPEC oil embargos of the 1970s was a reference point for what a future with insufficient oil supplies would look like. High oil prices would cause global inflation. A higher proportion of consumption spending would go directly or indirectly to energy. Economic output would decline and unemployment in developed countries would soar.

Iraq offered the best opportunity in the world for the West to discover new oil reserves. The country is about the size of Texas, but at the time of the Gulf War, it had only 2,300 wells vs. about one million in Texas. Iraq had great potential for new oil discoveries but didn't have the expertise to implement new technologies like 3-D seismic exploration and either deep or horizontal drilling.[65] Many people feared that after the 1991 war, Hussein would offer oil concessions to China and other countries that were not part of the Gulf War Coalition. How could Western companies get access to Iraqi oil?

In 1991, George H. W. Bush's critics believed that it was necessary to overthrow Saddam Hussein and forcibly acquire Iraq's oil reserves. A preemptive strike would give the United States and its allies access to new energy supplies; but the takeover would be more subtle than simply installing a US-led government. The Sunni dictator would be replaced by a Shiite Muslim regime that would gratefully grant Western companies oil concessions. This strategy was known as "regime change." But as Dick Cheney indicated in 1994, the George H. W. Bush administration felt that the risks of invading Baghdad were too great.

Flash-forward to 2003. Globalization was dramatically increasing demand for energy, so the George W. Bush administration's concerns about peak oil were greater than ever. The rapidly growing global economy was in fact putting millions of new cars on the road, especially in China and India. As predicted, new oil discoveries couldn't keep up with the increased demand for gasoline. Shale fracking was being used to produce natural gas, but hadn't yet been applied to oil production. The technology for deep-water drilling in the Gulf of Mexico was still in its infancy and was extremely expensive. Those who were concerned about peak oil feared that an energy shortage would bring back the stagflation of the 1970s and early 1980s.

In 2005, things got even scarier when a conservative American investment banker and Bush family friend, Matthew Simmons, wrote *Twilight in the Desert: The Coming Saudi Oil Shock and the World Economy*.[66] Simmons studied technical engineering reports that, he said, indicated that the world's largest oil exporter, Saudi Arabia, had far fewer oil reserves than it claimed. All signs seemed to point to a future world oil shortage.

Unlike most other members of their administration, both President George W. Bush and Vice President Dick Cheney had worked in the oil industry and knew about the very real possibility of a future shortfall in global oil supply. In the long run, overthrowing Hussein and protecting the West from an energy shortage would make them look like geniuses.

After 9/11, the United States destroyed the al-Qaeda training camp in Afghanistan. Then, rather strangely, the Bush administration invaded Afghanistan and injected American troops into a country with a long history of tribal disputes and weak central governments. But this odd decision to invade Afghanistan put troops on the ground in the Middle East. The rumors of WMDs made the invasion of Iraq look like only an incremental step in the war on terrorism.

American troops were now in a position to capture valuable Iraqi oil fields. But nothing went as planned. The Bush administration was shocked and awed at Iraqi resistance from every direction: Sunnis, Shiites, foreign al-Qaeda fighters, even local hooligans, all attacked the invading Americans. War raged until 2011 when there was a sufficient illusion of victory to bring the troops home.

If there was concern about a global energy shortage as far back as 1991, why weren't the American people informed? This important issue was public knowledge but almost never discussed. Liberal politicians and environmentalists didn't want to acknowledge the oil industry's economic importance. Besides, dramatically higher energy costs would make renewable forms of energy more economical. Conservative free market advocates always assured everyone that if we just "let the market handle it," then all would be well. But from 1991 to 2003, the near-religious nature of free market ideology precluded any open discussion of the real possibility that market forces themselves could create a worldwide economic downturn as bad as the Great Depression.

Rand Paul Doesn't Buy It

It's certainly possible that none of the alternative motives discussed earlier in this chapter had any bearing on the decision to go back to war in Iraq in 2003. Perhaps the war was caused by sheer incompetence. But the controversy over why we interrupted the war on terrorism to attack Iraq again has raged within the Republican Party for years.

In a speech at Western Kentucky University on April 7, 2009, just prior to announcing his senatorial bid, Republican Rand Paul accused Dick Cheney of fabricating an excuse to overthrow Saddam Hussein in order to benefit the oil industry. Cheney's former employer, Halliburton, had gotten a billion-dollar no-bid Defense Department contract at the beginning of the 2003 Iraq War. Paul invoked President Dwight Eisenhower's warnings that the military-industrial complex could direct American policy for its own economic benefit.

Rand Paul described the previously mentioned interview in which Dick Cheney gave numerous reasons for not invading Baghdad during the 1991 Gulf War. Paul then said, "That's why the first Bush didn't go into Baghdad. Dick Cheney then goes to work for Halliburton. Makes hundreds of millions of dollars, their CEO. Next thing you know, he's back in government and it's a good idea to go into Iraq."[67]

Nearly 4,500 American military personnel were among the more than one hundred thousand people who died in Iraq. Most of the deaths were innocent Iraqi civilians. Since there was no reliable evidence of weapons of mass destruction, it was reasonable to seek an alternative explanation of why we went back to Iraq.

No doubt that is what prompted Rand Paul's speculation about the cause of the war.

By the time Rand Paul gave his speech, shale fracking had begun to eliminate concerns about a worldwide energy shortage. Future Senator Paul came on the scene late and couldn't appreciate earlier Republican angst over peak oil. His suggestion that Dick Cheney was acting on behalf of Halliburton and other contractors was preposterous. But Paul was trying to find some rationale for a foreign policy decision in the George W. Bush administration that didn't seem to make any sense.

Beware What You Wish For

When terrible mistakes are made, it can be hard to predict the consequences. Overthrowing Saddam Hussein removed an effective barrier between Iran to the east and the other Middle East hotspots to the west (Syria, Lebanon, the Gaza Strip, the West Bank, and Israel). This dramatically increased Iran's influence in the area. Hussein's Sunni regime was initially replaced by a brutal Shiite regime. This led to the creation of al-Qaeda in Iraq, a branch of the Sunni terrorist organization, al-Qaeda. Later, al-Qaeda in Iraq would morph into ISIS, the Islamic State of Iraq and Syria, an organization with more power and greater ambitions than Osama bin Laden's original al-Qaeda.

ISIS would spread its influence from Libya in North Africa to Pakistan and use high-tech propaganda to attract impressionable followers from all over the world. This greatly magnified the threat of global terrorism. The second Iraq war was initially irrelevant to the war on terrorism and thus likely to be pointless. But the creation of ISIS made the war counterproductive. The United States left Iraq in 2011 but was forced to return in 2014 when American fighter jets were used to support Iraqi

Kurds, Shiites, and Sunnis fighting against ISIS. Thus began the third Iraq war.

Oil companies from the United States and other nations would eventually get their oil concessions from the newly installed Shiite regime in Iraq, but that too was pointless. By then, shale fracking had changed the world's oil markets.

In sum, Reaganomics as an economic policy always fails, but the same ideology wielded as a political strategy and supported by certain propaganda techniques has been effective at getting votes. Sadly, these same tactics were used in 2003 to create a pretext for a deadly war.

With nearly 4,500 American deaths and more than 31,400 serious injuries and a full-cycle cost of somewhere between $1 trillion and $3 trillion, the 2003 war in Iraq served no useful purpose except as a metaphor for what is wrong with American politics. The war was created by political extremists who, along with their predecessors going back to the 1930s, have been out of step with both the American people and economic reality. Since the 1980s, they have used deception, appealing fantasies, and the popularity of Ronald Reagan to inflict a string of disasters on the United States for the sole purpose of gaining political advantage. (The S&L crisis, the Great Recession, huge increases in the national debt, neglect of Hurricane Katrina survivors, mockery of all aspects of the American government, and finally, war.) Since 2003, their tactics have had an actual body count.

Chapter 11
Dissension and Chaos

FDR's New Deal programs in the 1930s made Democrats the nation's dominant political party. Roosevelt's aggressive policies in the Great Depression were viewed as more sympathetic to the needs of the people than anything the Republicans had to offer. LBJ's Great Society initiatives reinforced the Democrats' image as the party with domestic policies more compatible with the requirements of a modern economy. This was the status quo until the so-called Reagan Revolution of the 1980s. After that, Reaganomics' total failure as economic policy (chapters 7–9) made Democratic policies more acceptable again, right? Wrong!

Democrats were as confused as Republicans about what ended stagflation in the 1980s. They couldn't overcome the heavily promoted illusion that Ronald Reagan took office after Jimmy Carter and then, thanks to Reaganomics, the nation's economy magically turned around. It was even harder to overcome Reagan's personal popularity. Conservatives proudly called themselves Reagan Republicans. Jimmy Carter Democrats were scarcer than dodo birds. To add to the confusion, the United States enjoyed an extended period of relative prosperity from 1981 through 2000 (chapter 8). Neither Democrats nor anyone else understood that this economic bliss existed despite, and not because of, Reaganomics.

Republicans were relentlessly on message, saturating the media with antigovernment noise and distractions (chapter 10). Anyone could get elected in gerrymandered congressional districts simply by proclaiming their opposition to the American government in Washington, their preference for paying public bills with borrowed money instead of tax revenue, and their eagerness to let business interests operate without regulation. Democrats had no rebuttal. In fact, they were penalized for their historical use of government to overcome inadequacies in the markets—inadequacies that prevented people from obtaining the necessities of life.

In the Clinton administration, Democrats caved. It was politically expedient to simply go along. They could always fall back on arguments for increasing government efficiency, the need for market incentives, the importance of eliminating bureaucracy, everyone's desire to pay less taxes, and the burdens of business regulations. They attempted to cooperate with Republicans. Bill Clinton even proclaimed that the era of big government was over. Meanwhile, interference with government was working too well for Republicans who used it to get elected and reelected by claiming that government was dysfunctional.

When Barack Obama took office, he had to deal with disasters that stemmed from eight years of Reaganomics-style economic policies and two nebulous wars under George W. Bush. Yet Republicans in Congress were still able to obscure a thirty-plus-year train wreck of failed economic theories and blame Obama for everything. He was declared a big-government liberal as soon as he took office, and antigovernment conservatives treated every Obama proposal accordingly. They even objected to his 2009 stimulus plan and his creation of the Consumer Financial Protection Bureau, programs designed to ease the pain and prevent the recurrence, respectively, of the Great Recession.

After his 2012 reelection, the famously laid-back Obama seemed to throw up his hands in frustration. He became less inclined to humor the constant obstructionism from the dominant anti–American government faction of the GOP. When necessary,

Obama used his executive authority in an effort to get things done. For example, when a Republican-controlled Congress would not work with him to tackle the complex, bipartisan issue of immigration reform, Obama tried to use his powers as president to prevent the deportation of hundreds of thousands of young immigrants who had been in the United States all their lives.

Obama seemed to be less effective in his second term. But it is difficult to make a fair assessment since no other president has ever had to battle as many extremist groups (al Qaeda, ISIS, Hezbollah, far right-wing Republicans) at the same time. Each of these groups knew that it alone had the right answers, and wouldn't tolerate any disagreement. If Republicans couldn't get their way, then there would be no way. Not even in the run-up to the Civil War were there as many overt efforts in Congress to impede the routine functions of the American government.

By Obama's second term, Democratic voters had become disgusted with all the bickering, nonsensical talk, and distractions. Washington couldn't seem to run a government capable of meeting the needs of the people, needs that give rise to the five categories in chapter 1. Meanwhile, Republican voters voiced their contempt for government and readily supported presidential candidates who echoed their anger.

Some states even cut taxes and reduced public services. But this "race to the bottom" only increased the suffering of millions of Americans still trying to recover from the George W. Bush recession. Frustration with government reached a boiling point. The antigovernment strategy was working beautifully.

Change could come from only one source, that large majority of the population that had suffered needlessly from policies designed to thwart economic reality. Too many Americans had lost houses or jobs, found it impossible to send their kids to college without incurring massive debt, were burdened with inadequate employment, or felt disgusted with elected officials who seemed to favor absurd disparities of income and wealth. Something had to give!

The 99 Percent

Ironically, the financial sector greed that caused the Great Recession would open the door to changes in the way many people viewed economic policy. Reagan Republicans had labeled high-income and wealthy people "producers" and thus especially worthy of tax cuts. This included many in the financial sector whose actions had caused the mortgage lending and securitization problems that came to a head in 2007. It seemed that the most worthy among us had wrecked the economy.

Too little government financial regulation in the George W. Bush administration had allowed, even encouraged, the Wall Street activity that had brought the nation's economy to its knees. Bush reacted to the crisis by bailing out financial firms with the TARP program; but relief for ordinary Americans would only come in the Obama administration. By 2011, those ordinary Americans were no longer just reacting to the effects of the Great Recession; they began to address the cause.

So many people suffered during the Great Recession that, inevitably, social activists organized to protest against the financial sector. On September 17, 2011, the Occupy Wall Street movement took over Zuccotti Park in the New York City financial district. OWS was part of a worldwide movement protesting greed, maldistribution, and excessive corporate influence in government. It claimed that 99 percent of the American population suffered at the hands of the richest 1 percent.

Other Occupy Wall Street protests popped up around the

country and got plenty of media attention. But most Americans simply went about their business. Although many of them had been devastated by the downturn, they were not the activist sort. Besides, they were being constantly bombarded with shouts of "freedom" and other propaganda slogans designed to appeal to their natural antigovernment bias.

For many people, Democrats in particular, the damage was simply too great to ignore.

But a division developed within the Democratic Party between members offended by the disaster of Reaganomics, and Democrats from the Clinton administration seen as too close to Wall Street. In a strange way, this was the mirror image of the GOP split in the 1960s. Goldwater conservatives had broken with Republicans who acknowledged that there were necessary economic uses for government in a modern economy.

A feature article in a July 20, 2015, *Time* issue describes this disagreement among Democrats. It also includes some of the perpetually damning facts that stem from the antigovernment assault on America since 1980: "Real wages have increased 138 percent for the top 1 percent of American income earners since 1979," yet the overwhelming majority of Americans have experienced little or no gain. From 2002 to 2013, the only groups of American households that did not see their real incomes on average decline or stagnate were those headed by college graduates or by young people in their twenties. But for "over a quarter-century, fixed costs such as housing, education, and health care have outpaced inflation."[68]

After Barry Goldwater's disastrous 1964 loss to Lyndon Johnson, it took Republicans sixteen years to finally achieve acceptance of an alternative view of government. Unfortunately, Reaganomics proved to be horribly destructive to the nation. With overwhelming evidence that Reaganomics always fails, how long will it take Democrats, independents, and willing Republicans to accept the fact that government has an important role to play in the economy, a role that allows more people a reasonable chance to achieve the American dream?

Parties to Change

All but a comparatively few Americans have been harmed by Reaganomics. Several large groups of people have particularly compelling reasons to actively push for change. These groups overlap but together make up a significant majority of the nation's population.

Young people will inherit the federal debt created by their elders who cut taxes, refused to pay their bills, and crashed the economy with insufficient regulation, all while using government to spend massive amounts of money. The older generations have a clever way to escape their debt obligations: they will die. That won't help their children, who will never again make the mistake of having such irresponsible people for parents.

High school graduates find postsecondary education less affordable than ever. Yet many antigovernment politicians advocate reducing public support for higher education in favor of market solutions that don't actually exist. Officials in some states eagerly cede the authority to raise the costs of tuition and fees at public institutions to college presidents. Even though it is in the national interest to have an educated and well-trained population, students themselves are increasingly left to bear the extra costs. As a result, they find themselves relying more and more on borrowed money. Since education loans cannot be discharged in bankruptcy, there is no shortage of lenders. Creditors like the idea that they can hound former students for student loan payments forever.

As a result of shortsighted public policies, student loan obligations have risen to become the second-largest form of debt in the United States after home mortgage lending. This has a widespread effect on the national economy. We want people to finish their postsecondary school education, get jobs, and then spend money on cars, clothes, housing, pizza, beer, and other things in the real economy. Instead they are burdened by payments to the financial sector. This contributes to lower demand, reduces business activity, and stifles employment. As a result, the nation does not get the full benefit from the billions of dollars invested in education.

Millennials (Americans born between the early 1980s and the early 2000s) have been adversely impacted for years by decades of failed economic policy—i.e., Reaganomics. Moreover, they have lived all their lives in an environment in which extremists have sought political advantage by making a mockery of the American government. But it doesn't have to be like this; America can restore the prosperity enjoyed by previous generations. Millennials must overcome their understandable skepticism and vote to establish public policies that conform to the requirements of a modern economy.

Low-income people are the most severely affected by antigovernment policies. Chapter 1 described how inadequate employment prevents people from providing themselves with the necessities of life. We will discuss inadequate employment in more detail in chapter 13. For now, we simply note that this market-determined problem can only be directly alleviated by Category III (predominant market insufficiency) and Category IV (acute market insufficiency) functions of government.

No one can deny that good health is important. In the US economy, health insurance is typically the first step toward getting medical care. Yet there has been an extraordinary effort by those who oppose government to keep people from getting medical insurance. Since people with health problems cannot be expected to work and support themselves, an assault on Category IV functions like Medicaid and the Affordable Care Act is inconsistent with the conservative principle of personal responsibility.

Many members of America's growing elderly population often share the problems of both the poor and the sick. Though Medicare (Category I) and Social Security (Category III) have been monumentally important in improving the plight of senior citizens, the nation faces rapidly rising costs for nursing home care and for those afflicted with cognitive problems like Alzheimer's disease.

People will not let loved ones with treatable illnesses lie down and die for no reason, just to maintain the fantasy that markets can handle all our economic problems. Even Americans who vote for antigovernment policies expect Grandma and Grandpa to be taken care of in moments of extreme need.

Women could be the key to ending the partisan bickering in Washington that routinely produces either gridlock or policies that work to the detriment of most Americans. The "New Girls Club" of elected women in Congress has been more effective at getting things done than the "Old Boys Club." After the 2014 elections, there were a record 104 women serving in Congress. Their willingness to work across the aisle proved critical in October 2015 when Republicans opposed to Obamacare threatened to shut down government. Senators Kelly Ayotte (R-NH), Susan Collins (R-ME), Barbara Mikulski (D-MD), Lisa Murkowski (R-AK), and Patty Murray (D-WA) joined forces to shame the US Congress into hammering out a budget.

Women are quicker to understand the need for government functions that are the difference between life and death for many people. Across the nation, many women make less money than men, typically have more responsibility for children, and often live closer to the edge of economic disaster. For them, public economic policy that maintains adequate government services is neither an abstraction nor a political football.

Disgruntled Republicans

An often-abused segment of the political class, so-called "Establishment Republicans" suffer the daily humiliation of watching extremists in their own party push economic policies that invariably do damage to the nation. The traditional conservative Republicans who have managed to hang on while those around them are losing their heads can play a huge role in establishing good government and rational economic policies.

In recent years, far right-wing Republicans have masked extremist tendencies in their party by selecting a moderate presidential candidate. Barry Goldwater's ultraconservative campaign and subsequent landslide loss to Lyndon Johnson in 1964 serve as perpetual warnings to Republicans. However, selecting moderate candidates can sometimes have bizarre consequences.

In 2008, Republican presidential candidate John McCain chose Alaska governor Sarah Palin as his vice presidential running mate. Palin was a favorite of GOP extremists but was woefully unprepared on national and international issues. Prominent historian Robert Caro said that "McCain's selection of Sarah Palin is the single most irresponsible act of government I can remember."[69]

In 2012, moderate Republican presidential candidate Mitt Romney was forced to repudiate his greatest achievement as governor of Massachusetts, a statewide health-care plan that became the model for Democratic president Barack Obama's Affordable Care Act.*

Because of its opposition to regulation, the business community has been a reliable source of support for Republican candidates. It has provided both political contributions and separate, well-funded media campaigns favorable to the GOP. But business interests who sowed the wind, reaped the whirlwind in 2013, when division among Republican extremists caused a pointless government shutdown that cost the nation $24 billion in economic activity. This "schism within a schism" in the Republican Party showed that ideological purists would attack government even at the expense of private sector markets. This so riled up the US Chamber of Commerce that many of its members subsequently switched their support to more rational elements of the GOP.

Establishment Republicans frequently find themselves at odds with GOP members holding outlandish views on immigration, voting rights, and Congress. The modern Tea Party's opposition to taxes has nothing in common with eighteenth-century Tea Party protestors who famously opposed "taxation without representation." The Boston Tea Party participants understood the obvious need for some taxation, but insisted on a voice in the

---

*   The Democrats advocated either a single-payer health insurance system (Medicare for all) or the option for people under sixty-five to buy into Medicare. But when Barack Obama began a push for health-care reform in 2010, some Democrats refused to support either Democratic plan. This threatened what was destined to be a close vote in Congress. Much to the irritation of many Democrats, the president offered a plan modeled after Romney's system in Massachusetts. Obama's plan included two key Republican ideas, insurance mandates and an insurance exchange that allowed price comparisons. The Affordable Care Act is substantially a Republican plan. But rather than cooperate in health-care reform, the GOP sought political advantage by complaining about big government. They derided the plan as "Obamacare."

imposition of taxes. By contrast, modern protestors have objected to tax laws enacted by elected representatives who are the voice of the people. These antidemocratic views appalled more moderate Republicans, who saw the obvious need for government functions, all of which are funded by taxation.

Chaos

Since 1980, decades of increasing nonsense, misinformation, and distractions (chapter 10) have addled many voters to the point that they are unable to make rational choices. The default position for some people has become a preference for presidential candidates who have never previously held public office; that is, candidates whose sole qualification is that voters have not yet made the mistake of electing them.

By 2015, widespread opposition to government had spread all across the country. It is important to understand the nature of this resistance, lest we forget that the public sector is absolutely critical to the proper functioning of a modern economy.

One group, made up mostly of Democrats and frustrated Independents, was angry at federal and state governments because the public sector was not providing the five categories of government services that are so important in a modern economy. This group was actually complaining about too little government. Their problem was that Republican extremists had been so successful in their refusal to govern in good faith that they had clogged up the machinery of government.

Another group, even angrier and louder, had voted for the extremist politicians who were making a mockery of government. Antigovernment voters had elected people who promised to go to Washington and get the federal government "off their backs" by keeping it from working. When this tactic succeeded, these voters couldn't understand why everything was going wrong. Since the 1980s, their opposition to taxes has increased the national debt while their support for less business regulations also caused major problems. Many of these antigovernment voters still suffered from the lingering effects of the Great Recession, an economic disaster enabled by antiregulatory policies in the George W. Bush administration.

All across the country, people were hurting. Even improvements in the American economy during the Obama administration were misleading. Reduced unemployment hid the effects of income maldistribution. In 2014, there were 46.7 million people living below the poverty level, a record.[70] When the effects of inadequate employment are added, even more people than that are suffering.

Democrats were frustrated that political opposition to government programs made public sector solutions impossible. Even when government worked—the Affordable Care Act, for example, had reduced the share of uninsured Americans from 13.3 percent in 2013 to 10.4 percent in 2014—there were constant threats to eliminate successful programs.[71]

Meanwhile, confused antigovernment voters in the Republican Party were shifting their support to fresh faces like Donald Trump, Dr. Ben Carson, and Carly Fiorina. But even the fresh faces largely advocated failed polices like Reaganomics. Amid all the wailing and gnashing of teeth, one fact stood out. The anti–American government faction of the GOP still tacitly accepted the notion that the American majority was incapable of running their government for their own benefit.

Many Americans did seem to be increasingly unworthy of democracy. They had forgotten the three axioms of governance in America, three facts that will not go away. First, the US

Constitution mandates a system of checks and balances designed to thwart a takeover by some aspiring monarch. This fear has largely subsided, but we are left with a federal government that can only function properly if officials act in good faith. This is impossible if we keep electing people who promise to act in bad faith and undermine government.

Second, the first four categories of government functions described in chapter 1 are not optional; they are requirements of a modern economy. There is no reason that people should be deprived of the necessities of life because of market deficiencies. Government is an intrinsic part of our economic system, and that system must work properly if people are to survive.

Finally, the American people are united only by what they do together through their government. Of all nationalities, Americans are the most diverse group of people in the world. They differ in every way: politics, religious beliefs, economic status, cultural and linguistic backgrounds, and in their interpretations of the Constitution and the Bill of Rights. The American government is literally the only thing that binds them together and makes them a nation. No functional government means no United States of America.

In the 2016 presidential election, large numbers of confused and angry Americans made their frustrations known. They were fed up with dysfunctional government, "politics as usual," inadequate employment, budget deficits, the high cost of higher education and medical care, and the people that they had elected to public offices. The policies that they had voted for since the 1980s had backfired on them. Billionaires and socialists rushed to their rescue.

People *in extremis* politically seemed to bounce back and forth across the ideological spectrum. An article in the February

8, 2016, issue of *Time* magazine indicated that shortly before the Iowa caucuses, many newly active voters were torn between billionaire capitalist Donald Trump and avowed socialist senator Bernie Sanders. What was happening in America?

All these disaffected voters have two things in common, and this suggests a way to solve America's economic and political problems. First, most of the economic problems that beset them are caused by the *failures* of Reaganomics as economic policy. Second, the dysfunctional government they complain about is entirely due to the *success* of Reaganomics as political strategy. This should provide guidance for future changes in public policy, a topic that will be addressed in full in part IV.

Meanwhile, the nation can reflect on the greatest irony in American history: Reaganomics is not the solution; Reaganomics is the problem.

Chapter 12
Reagan's Legacy

Every application of Reaganomics has failed at every level of government. This shouldn't surprise us, since any attempt to defy reality invites failure. American economic history reveals why Ronald Reagan had an uphill battle in his attempts to defy the requirements of a modern economy.

Since the early days of the republic, government, taxation, and regulation have all increased for pragmatic reasons. As inadequacies in the private sector markets became evident, voters naturally pooled their resources through government and solved any problems that arose. Americans throughout history have insisted on more security, food safety, infrastructure, education, and other public services. Only foolish people would do without the necessities of life (e.g., roads, bridges, a water and sewage system, national defense, police protection, regulations mandating food safety, universal education, etc.) just because no one can make a buck providing them.

By the very early twentieth century, the United States had experienced the depredations of the Standard Oil Trust, feared contaminated food after reading Upton Sinclair's *The Jungle*, and seen the need for expanded public infrastructure as the nation's population grew. If Reaganomics ever had any economic applications, the requirements of a modern economy were rapidly making it obsolete even before Ronald Reagan (1911–2004) was born. This didn't stop Reagan's followers from using this failed theory for political gain.

Reagan vs. the Modern Republican Party

Reaganomics as a political strategy (chapter 10) has proven to be an irresistible temptation to many politicians. It allows them

to toss misconceptions, distractions, and noise into a public relations blender and extract whatever is necessary to get votes or
to justify failed policies. When enough people believe nonsense,
then nonsense becomes public policy.

Would Ronald Reagan himself have approved of all the political shenanigans done in his name by self-proclaimed "Reagan
Republicans"? Not according to former Republican senator and
presidential candidate Bob Dole who, in a 2013 interview, said
that the GOP should hang a "closed for repairs" sign on its doors
until it came up with some positive ideas. Dole claimed that today,
Reagan wouldn't feel comfortable in his own political party.[72]

It is both ironic and tragic that thanks to some of his followers,
Ronald Reagan himself became the Trojan horse who brought
destructive politics through the gates of his "Shining City on a Hill."
Reagan's image and reputation became indispensable political
tools that, along with distractions and misinformation, were used
to promote economic policies that damaged the nation. If, to use
the Vietnam War–era expression, antigovernment politicians had
to destroy the country in order to save it, then so be it.

Reagan was a far more complex person than modern Republicans realize. During the Great Depression, he saw that the means
of survival for many Americans could be derailed by circumstances beyond their control. Like most Americans at the time,
Reagan's family benefited from FDR's New Deal. So not surpris-
ingly, Reagan was initially a liberal Democrat. He supported
collective bargaining, joined the Screen Actors Guild, and later
became the union's president.

Reagan's conservative shift came as a response to allegations
of Communist influence in Hollywood. Even then, he expressed
views than were far more liberal than most Americans when he
said, "As a citizen I would hesitate, or not like, to see any political

party outlawed on the basis of its political ideology."[73] Reagan's conservatism hardened when as governor of California he had to deal with unruly college students. Reagan had no patience with protests that broke the law, a fact amply illustrated after he became president and fired air traffic controllers engaged in an illegal strike.

The Reagan Paradox: The Conservative Icon and Today's GOP, a collection of essays from friends and writers familiar with Reagan, was published in 2014 on the tenth anniversary of Reagan's death. *Time* magazine's Alex Altman nicely summed up the differences between Reagan and the increasingly dominant antigovernment wing of the Republican Party that so disturbed Bob Dole. Altman noted that Reagan "proposed the largest tax hike by any governor in the history of the United States. As president, he raised taxes eleven times, never submitted a balanced budget request, hiked the debt ceiling eighteen times and bemoaned the congressional brinkmanship that 'consistently brings the government to the edge of default before facing its responsibility.' Plus, the federal deficit nearly tripled."[74] Moreover,

> Reagan was a onetime union leader who extolled the virtues of collective bargaining. As governor of California, he championed environmental legislation and signed a bill making it easier to get an abortion. The only U.S. president to divorce, he incensed the Christian right by nominating a socially moderate judge, the future swing vote Sandra Day O'Connor, to serve on the Supreme Court. He cut sweeping deals with liberal legislators like Tip O'Neill, the Democratic speaker of the House. He signed a major overhaul of the U.S. immigration system than ultimately granted amnesty to some 3 million undocumented immigrants.[75]

One can speculate what Ronald Reagan would have said about today's Republican Party had he lived longer and stayed in good health. As a patriotic American and a responsible conservative, Reagan would likely have spoken out against politically motivated government shutdowns and economic policies that consistently harm most Americans.

Making Lemons Out of Lemonade

Ronald Reagan was easily the luckiest president in American history. Widespread confusion helped get him elected the first time, and the timing of events beyond his control got him reelected. But Reagan's own domestic policies caused turmoil in the financial sector, unnecessary budget deficits, and a huge increase in the national debt.

Other than the INF Treaty that he and Soviet premier Mikhail Gorbachev had agreed to, Reagan had little if any foreign policy accomplishments. He often seemed to be lost unless he could deal with people face-to-face. The unnecessary deaths of 241 American servicemen in Lebanon after a 1982 suicide bombing and the 1986 Iran-Contra scandal greatly tarnished Reagan's image. The latter might have been grounds for impeachment for a less popular president.

Despite Reagan's lack of accomplishments, there was a degree of public sympathy. Ronald Reagan was the oldest president in the nation's history, and by the end of his second term, the deterioration was becoming evident. Even when he denied being out of the loop, the public readily assumed that Reagan may not have fully understood what was going on during the Iran-Contra Affair.

Looking back, the Reagan administration was mainly eight years of sound bites and photo ops. There was Reagan with

Gorbachev, Reagan with Tip O'Neill, Reagan with British prime minister Margaret Thatcher, and Reagan with Reagan. There was Reagan with jokes and quips and antigovernment rhetoric, the larval stage of modern Republican Party politics. And there was the tacit complicity of Democrats, who were beginning a long period of irrelevancy.

There was, above all, failed economic policy, a precursor of things to come. Few understood the implications of inadequate financial regulations in the Reagan years, which enabled the S&L crisis and the LBO problems on Wall Street. With hindsight, the Great Recession was almost inevitable. But in the 1980s, people reveled in "freedom" and tax cuts and budget deficits. Reagan had brought optimism. All was right with the world.

A Realistic View of Reagan's Presidency

Ronald Reagan couldn't bequeath Americans his extraordinary good luck; he left only Reaganomics, both as an economic policy and a political strategy. We see the implications of this in the very different fates of the two Bush presidents.

Republican George H. W. Bush had rejected Reaganomics in 1980 as an unworkable economic theory that he famously called "voodoo economics." He resisted the temptation to say "I told you so" when, as president, his main domestic achievement was to clean up the wreckage of his predecessor, Ronald Reagan. Bush's refusal to drink the Reaganomics Kool-Aid and a bit of bad luck (Ross Perot and a slight recession) cost him reelection in 1992— this despite his superlative leadership during both the collapse of the Soviet Union and the 1991 Gulf War. George H. W. Bush was probably the best president since Franklin Roosevelt.

His son, Republican George W. Bush, accepted Reaganomics and gave us tax cuts and budget deficits, inadequate financial regulation and the Great Recession, and neglect of Hurricane Katrina victims ("government is not the solution; government is the problem"). This, combined with his nebulous nation-building efforts in Afghanistan and a deadly and counterproductive war in Iraq, made the second Bush the worst president in American history—by orders of magnitude. If Americans learned anything at all from his administration's failures, then no future president is likely to challenge Bush for that dubious distinction. Historians have a long memory. Hopefully, they will warn the country if some future president sets off on a George W. Bush–like trajectory.

The world leader most often compared to Ronald Reagan was conservative British prime minister Margaret Thatcher. Under the parliamentary system, the "Iron Lady" was forced out of Ten Downing Street in 1990 by her own political party. The Tories couldn't take the heat of public revulsion at Thatcher's version of Reaganomics.

So how do we rate Ronald Reagan? Nothing Reagan accomplished domestically mitigates the damage done by the S&L crisis, the LBO fiasco, and his huge peacetime budget deficits. In fact, his "feel-good" economic policies remind us of Republicans' long-standing complaints about Democrats. In foreign policy, the Reagan-Gorbachev INF Treaty was important, but so were the Iran-Contra Affair and the unnecessary loss of American lives in Lebanon.

Despite his good luck Reagan was, at best, a mediocre president. If he is deemed to have some culpability for the subsequent disasters that Reaganomics inflicted upon the nation, then he was unquestionably a below-average president. The Republican Party's continued "positive" use of Reagan's name, image, and mythology is simply an application of Reaganomics as a political strategy.

Americans who cheered for Ronald Reagan when he took office in 1981—those who were present at the devolution—reveled in the sense of optimism that the handsome onetime actor brought to the presidency. Everyone seemed to like Ronald Reagan and wanted to believe everything he said. But personal popularity cannot compensate for bad policies. Reaganomics as economic policy has proven to be useful only as a guide for what *not* to do in a modern economy. Reaganomics as political strategy has encouraged antigovernment tactics that routinely lapse into sedition.

Noted British historian J. M. Roberts will have the last word on Reagan. In the eighth edition (1993) of his *History of the World*, Roberts wrote that Reagan survived the Iran-Contra Affair "as a remarkably popular figure; only after he had left office did it begin to dawn that for most Americans the decade had been one in which they had got poorer. Only rich Americans got richer during the Reagan presidency."[76]

*   *   *

Despite a steady reduction in the unemployment rate after the Great Recession, most Americans have continued to struggle. The overwhelming majority have found it more difficult to provide themselves and their families with the long list of necessities required by our modern economy. Inadequate employment is rampant, and neglect of government has taken a toll as infrastructure crumbles and the national debt increases. Postsecondary education and training have become less obtainable. People with skills unsuited to our modern technology- and capital-intensive economy drop out of the workforce, while high-skilled jobs go unfilled due to lack of sufficient education and training. Huge amounts of energy and political capital are expended to deprive people of health insurance. Continuous assaults on government threaten to reduce both public sector services and government jobs, services and jobs that are not available from the private sector. Incredibly, some people get elected to office by promising to keep the system from working.

The biggest domestic issue in twenty-first-century America is the neglect of the American people and their government. In their own peculiar way, markets always work. But the people must take charge of everything else. In part IV, we'll use some of the most important concepts in modern economics (employment, trans-actions, and income and wealth distribution) to address market inadequacies and construct proper public policy in a modern economy. The failure of Reaganomics as economic policy is our guide for what *not* to do.

Part IV

Market Inadequacies: Pressure Points in a
Modern Economy

Chapter 13
Employment

Unlike their primitive ancestors, people in a modern economy do not have any realistic possibility of self-sufficiency. They must rely on an interconnected system of markets and government in order to survive. People must work to earn money in order to make purchases and pay taxes. The modern economy is virtually defined by the pervasive need for some form of paid employment.

But there are complications, especially the fact that the economy does not need everybody to work. Parents, for example, have almost always taken care of small children. Throughout history, all the people have always been supported by less than all the people. Over many centuries, progress (new inventions, increased efficiency, and better health care), prosperity, and compassion have greatly expanded the proportion of the population not expected to work.

In order to better understand employment's critical role in a modern economy, we will attempt to characterize every person's work status. This qualitative analysis begins by dividing the population into two components, the nonemployed (those not expected to work) and the labor force. We will find a place for everyone and put everyone in their place.

The Nonemployed
Half the people in America are nonemployed. We simply do not need everyone to work. The nonemployed includes children, most full-time students, retirees, the nonproductive rich, those with serious health problems (e.g., residents of nursing homes, assisted-living facilities, and hospices, as well as many seriously ill hospital patients), most of the homeless, and incarcerated

criminals. This population is characterized by its lack of productive output. Some, like retirees and students, may have part-time work. Prisoners may engage in work-related programs, such as making license plates. Homelessness is such a huge impediment to obtaining work that it often relegates some unfortunate people to nonemployed status.

Our distinction between the productive rich and the nonproductive rich merits some comment. People may acquire wealth in many ways: successful entrepreneurs create vast business empires, people inherit money or win the lottery, bigtime criminals may manage to avoid imprisonment, corporate executives receive massive compensation, and talented people in sports and in the arts and entertainment fields often make a lot of money. Once the money is obtained, wealthy people may at some time simply choose to stop working and cease to be productive. As we'll see in chapter 15, large fortunes can continue to grow and spin off considerable income without the owners' actual participation.

Some wealthy people deserve credit for contributing their labor and money to good causes in the community. They establish museums, lead efforts to beautify cities, and help fund social services for the needy. When these activities consume much time and effort, this population's volunteer work will distinguish them from the nonproductive wealthy who merely lead a life of leisure.

At some point, the nonproductive rich may declare themselves to be retired. Since a newly conceived heir may be assured of a great fortune, prenatal retirement is at least theoretically possible. All we know is that the productive status of the wealthy is a far more nebulous concept than most people realize.

We address the status of healthy people (male or female) who stay at home with considerable trepidation. Employment is defined not by explicit compensation, but by the production of goods or services. Certainly, stay-at-home parents watching children are employed. Childcare is an invaluable service.

There is little correlation between homemaking duties and the need to actually stay at home. Some two-income couples, either by choice or necessity, take care of all their domestic needs (housecleaning, cooking, yard maintenance, etc.) without assistance. On the other hand, there are people who stay at home and have no defined output, yet have a retinue of servants. We can only say that "homemaker" overlaps the employed and nonemployed categories.

One segment of the nonemployed population deserves special attention: incarcerated criminals. We lament the fact that they are supported by tax revenue. But incarceration is by far the most effective means of minimizing unemployment. The criminal justice system is the only part of the economy that provides massive numbers of jobs, all for the sole purpose of taking other people out of the labor force.

We don't need everybody to work, but the burden of involuntary unemployment will fall disproportionately on certain groups. Some people are discriminated against for reasons of race, religion, ethnicity, age, health, or physical appearance. Poor people may have a difficult time finding work. They have no financial resources for education and training, and they typically lack the business contacts that other people take for granted. Young people are especially vulnerable since they have little or no work experience. They may find it difficult to get internships and summer jobs that are often the first steps toward future employment.

Poor, idle, but energetic young people and those who are discriminated against will often grow tired of watching American affluence on television and, in the finest tradition of capitalism, will strike out on a life of crime. These entrepreneurial risk-takers will become drug dealers, rob convenience stores, steal ATMs, and break into homes. After all, money is essential in a modern economy.

They eventually get caught and wind up in the criminal justice system, providing jobs for others. If we ignore issues like fairness and decency, this is the most effective method devised by man for creating jobs for some while removing others from the unemployment lines. The very people whom no one wants to hire are conveniently taken out of circulation.

Ex-convicts have a tremendously difficult time getting a job and thus may be punished their whole lives for a single mistake. They effectively become members of the nonemployed. Perhaps people convicted of a single nonviolent offense should have their criminal records expunged after completing their punishment.

Currently, there are proposals from conservatives and liberals alike to reduce incarceration. Many of the 2.3 million people in US jails and prisons are there for either nonviolent offenses or for crimes committed when they were children. But a big decrease in the population of incarcerated criminals and a reduced number of jobs in the criminal justice system together risk creating a large net gain in unemployment. This increased unemployment would reduce aggregate demand, thus diminishing the job prospects for the former prison employees and newly released criminals.

The existence of a large population of nonemployed people is an inescapable fact of our modern economy. No demand goes unsatisfied because of their lack of output. Our economic system is fully capable of providing everything the nonemployed and the unemployed need. Those who boast about the virtues of the free enterprise system should not sit idly by while others suggest that markets are so inefficient that they can offer work to everyone who either wants or needs a job.

Some of the nonemployed may be able to support themselves, but many require public social services or charitable help. Often, the nonemployed are kept alive only by our compassion. Category IV functions of government such as food stamps and Medicaid satisfy needs that are created by market forces.

If we fully expect large numbers of people to be nonemployed, how do we pass judgment on those in the labor force who either cannot find work or who have inadequate employment? In a primitive economy, adults could simply get up in the morning and seek the necessities of life. In a modern economy, people must find some way to make money. But there is no inherent match between the number of people needed to work and the number of people whom we expect to work. The only things that we can definitively say is that because of market forces, we do not need everyone to work, and many of those who do work full-time will not be able to provide themselves with all the necessities of life.

The Labor Force

With apologies for using a double negative, the labor force consists of people who are not among the nonemployed, as defined earlier. The labor force consists both of people who are working and the unemployed. Unemployed members of the labor force lack any qualifying characteristics that would afford them nonemployed status, such as wealth, incarceration, health problems, and the pursuit of education.

The employed may have either adequate or inadequate employment. Recall that the latter describes jobs with some defect that, over the course of a lifetime in that job, will keep a worker from providing himself with all the necessities of life.

The unemployed may have transitional unemployment (they are between jobs) or intrinsic unemployment (they are not needed to work in their geographic area). Those who get discouraged and stop looking for jobs are either nonemployed (if they can support themselves from savings, trust funds, inheritance, cashing in their IRAs, or theft) or intrinsically unemployed, if they are supported by others. People seeking a job may think that they have transitional unemployment, but then find themselves out of work for prolonged periods due to forces beyond their control, such as a recession or the loss of jobs at a major employer in their community.

There are four categories in the labor force, and three of them are bad. People may have adequate employment (good), inadequate employment (bad), transitional unemployment (worse), or intrinsic unemployment (terrible). Employment status is mainly determined by market conditions, not by people. For example, unemployed laborers who lost their jobs during a downturn in the construction industry and unemployed earth scientists with multiple college degrees who lost their jobs during the latest slump in the oil industry, may find themselves in the same unemployment line.

If people encounter a prolonged period of unemployment, they may exhaust their limited resources. Bankruptcy, even homelessness, may follow. The risks can never be completely eliminated, but Americans can use government (e.g., unemployment compensation, food stamps) to mitigate the vagaries of the marketplace that threaten human survival. Destitute people in a modern economy cannot just escape to the wilderness and take up hunting and gathering.

Inadequate Employment

During the Obama administration, unemployment from the Great Recession was cut in half from a rate of just more than 10 percent to less than 5 percent. But for a variety of reasons, many Americans did not fully participate in the recovery. Some people lacked the education and training necessary to compete in a modern economy. Others were forced to retire early or otherwise drop out of the workforce. Since businesses are always looking for ways to increase efficiency by reducing labor costs, workers often found a shortage of good jobs and settled on poor jobs. Public policies since the 1980s that have favored the wealthy have done nothing for the bulk of the American population, a problem that will occupy most of the rest of this book.

The huge disparity in economic success between the "haves" and the "have-nots" has become the nation's biggest economic problem. Its source can be traced to pervasive inadequate employment. Many people are forced to live from check to check and may have to neglect some of the necessities of life even when working full-time. The first omission is typically retirement savings, followed by medical and dental care.

Low wages are a big part of the problem. In some areas of the country, only minimum wage laws protect employees from market-determined wages that might be as low as four dollars or five dollars per hour. Workers have no control of these market forces, and low pay makes it financially impossible for them to move to a better job market. Yet workers are routinely blamed for their plight.

Consider "Joe," a fast-food worker who fries hamburgers and makes a little above minimum wage with no benefits. The standard response to Joe's circumstances is that if he would just get off his butt and get more education, then he could support himself. Let's suppose Joe takes our advice. He graduates from college, goes to medical school, and ultimately becomes a neurosurgeon. Joe has solved his financial problems.

But note two things. First, Joe's replacement at the fast-food outlet is also making just above minimum wage with no benefits. Moreover, and pardon the hyperbole, if Joe gets tired of doing brain surgery and returns to his old job frying hamburgers, then even with two college degrees, he will again make just above minimum wage with no benefits. Clearly the job is the problem, not the employee.

Low wages aren't the only problem. Many workers complain about their inability to work sufficient hours to support themselves and their families. This problem has been greatly magnified in recent years by the use of scheduling techniques that require seemingly infinite flexibility by employees. Workers are kept on call, get assignments with short notice, work only a few hours at a time, and have irregular and unpredictable working lives. Just-in-time labor (people) is used as casually as just-in-time inventory (physical objects). This is all done for the convenience of the employer. But it interferes with family life and makes it impossible for people to hold second jobs or go to school to improve themselves.

The increased use of contract labor allows companies to avoid hiring people. Clerks, secretaries, receptionists, janitors, warehouse laborers, customer service workers, and many other people now do jobs as "temps." This allows companies to avoid employee benefits, workmen's compensation, and severance pay. Jobs that once provided careers for millions of Americans have been reduced to the status of inadequate employment.

Minimum wage legislation and laws that end exploitation of workers classified as contract labor are both important Category II functions of government. But for years, people who work for tips have been exempted from federally mandated minimum wage requirements. As a result, food servers with full-time jobs have often required public assistance like food stamps.

We encounter inadequate employment everywhere. A large store that is part of a grocery supermarket chain might have more than one hundred full- and part-time employees. Yet only the store manager and perhaps, at most, a few other people (assistant managers, accounting clerks, or butchers) have adequate employment. The rest, somewhere between 95 percent and 99 percent of the store's employees, have inadequate employment.

Adequate employment must include enough compensation to pay for more than just the primitive economy's list of basic necessities: food, clothing, and shelter. The need to work and function properly in an interconnected modern economy expands the list of necessities to include transportation, communication, education, medical care, retirement savings, and physical security. The income level to attain adequate employment status is considerably above the poverty level. The latter, $23,850 for a family of four in 2015, is not enough to survive without government assistance. So-called "entitlement" programs are necessary precisely because we have a market-based economy.

People with inadequate employment typically have jobs that cannot be outsourced to other countries. Yet all of them require the necessities of life. No doubt, they would also like to enjoy a few of the pleasures that our advanced economy has to offer.

Rent-Seeking Managers
Market purists tell us that people must live with their low wages; that's just the way markets work. Yet many of the highest-paid people in the country seem to escape market-determined compensation altogether. This can often be explained by a peculiar form of "rent-seeking" behavior.

The use or exploitation of certain resources such as land and mineral rights requires payments in the form of rents or royalties to the resource owners. These resources are finite and irreplaceable. Market forces determine the compensation—generically called "rent"—received by resource owners. This compensation is paid irrespective of the resource owner's efforts or whether they inherited or purchased the resource.

While the supply of land is fixed, it is possible to reduce the supply of certain types of labor, so that it will command higher compensation. Labor unions representing skilled craftsmen such as electricians and plumbers have a vested interest in high licensing standards, both to ensure expertise and to reduce competition. Part of the resulting "market-determined" wages consists of "rent" that these workers receive due to their ownership of a restricted resource, namely their own labor.

A variation of this rent-seeking behavior is common in high-level white-collar employment. Managers are often paid enormous sums for reasons that have nothing to do with either markets or their contributions to their employer's success. The relative scarcity of managers compared with the mass of ordinary workers creates the illusion that each manager is the possessor of a scarce skill set that should command high compensation. Perhaps more important, their earnings are determined by people like themselves who have a vested interest in an overall high level of executive compensation. In effect, corporate executives are paid a form of rent for their "position" in the company.

Why does an executive make $500,000 a year for what could easily be a good $250,000-a-year job? Even though he makes no contribution to the company's success that justifies the higher compensation, people just like him in the company agree to pay him that much. His employer made money before he got there; presumably, it will continue to do so despite the fact that he's an employee. But "positioning," or extra pay for having a title in the company hierarchy, is pervasive in the corporate world.

Executive pay rises most rapidly for external reasons such as increased sales and profits in a booming industry. This phenomenon, which has been called "pay for luck," is particularly evident in US corporations. Senior executives' having their "hand in the till" may be a more apt metaphor for modern corporate capitalism than Adam Smith's "invisible hand."[77]

There are reasons that the owners of a corporation, the shareholders, don't just simply replace overpaid executives with equally good people who will gladly work for less money. First, positioning is so pervasive in the business world that unreasonable compensation has become the norm in many high-level jobs. This is the source of much of the income disparity between the "haves" and the "have-nots" alluded to earlier. Also, corporations are run by managers and boards of directors who are very much part of the problem. They personally benefit from this "positioning."

Another factor contributing to absurd levels of executive compensation might be called "the mystery of large numbers." Consider a big corporation with $10 billion in annual revenue. If just 1 percent ($100 million) of the revenue is paid to the top twenty-five executives, then they receive an average of $4 million each. That's a lot of money; but it's only 1 percent of revenue! It is easy to hide excessive compensation in big numbers.

Our concerns about ultra-high levels of income and wealth in a modern economy have nothing to do with envy. All workers must have adequate employment in order to survive and, as we'll see in the next two chapters, huge disparities of income and wealth may increase the amount of money available for investment even as they reduce employment, consumption, demand, and opportunities for investment.

Public Policy Implications

The first four categories of government functions described in chapter 1 are not optional. They help provide necessities that are not adequately available from the private sector. When the public sector is allowed to perform its proper role in a modern economy, jobs are created that will not come from anywhere else. Many, if not most, of these jobs are in the private sector. Category V (General Market Insufficiency) addresses the remaining inadequacies in the marketplace and creates unique jobs as well.

Sometimes the empirical evidence for government pops up in surprising ways. Job openings in July 2015 compared with June soared 8 percent to 5.75 million even as total hiring declined. This apparent anomaly has been attributed to a shortage of skilled workers to fill "unique positions that didn't exist five to ten years ago."[78] The nation's cavalier attitude toward Category III functions of government (i.e., education and training) is beginning to show up in the workplace as it has become increasingly difficult for people to obtain the skills required by our modern economy.

This is not your great-great-great-grandfather's economy. We now know that markets alone will not solve all problems. Chapter 14 will reveal that employment is both increased and optimized when government performs its proper role in a modern economy to compensate for deficiencies in the private sector markets.

Chapter 14
Employment-Minimizing Transactions

Since lack of work is an existential threat to many people in a modern economy, we are interested in the impact of various kinds of transactions on employment. Money will either be spent or saved. Spending, or consumption, is the driving force in the economy and is the catalyst for productive activity, jobs, and investment. Savings are typically put in the financial sector, where they become available for investment. At first glance it seems that no matter where money goes, only good things happen. But it turns out that economic transactions are not all created equal. It matters where money goes.

Dynamic Products and Static Assets
Many people are employed in the manufacture of tangible products (goods) such as shirts, automobiles, and television sets. Food processing, for example, is often labor intensive. In the field of real estate, new home construction and sales require numerous craftsmen and laborers as well as white-collar workers such as real estate agents and mortgage bankers. We may define a *dynamic product* to be a good or service created for a transaction. All services are dynamic products. Sales of dynamic products, *dynamic transactions*, are characterized by their high labor content.

Alternatively, a transaction may involve the sale of an existing asset, a *static asset*, such as a used car, an already-built home, land, or shares of common stock in the secondary market. The sale of a static asset is a *static transaction*. Typically, static transactions have some dynamic component. Stockbrokers are paid to handle exchanges of existing shares and real estate agents make commissions selling existing homes. Since money is usually involved in a transaction, we characterize an exchange as either dynamic or static depending on whether more money is paid for the dynamic component or the static component.

Money itself is a static asset. Payments of interest and dividends are static transactions, mere movements of money from one place to another. This includes interest paid on the national debt. Sales of existing capital assets are also static transactions.

The desirability of dynamic transactions notwithstanding, there is nothing intrinsically wrong with static transactions. They range from buying items at a garage sale to the purchase of a Fortune 500 company; from the sale of modest homes to sales of Western ranches, Malibu beach houses, or Greenwich, Connecticut, estates; and from clunker used cars to vintage Bentleys. For now, we just note that most of the very biggest transactions in the economy, sales valued at millions or billions of dollars, are merely the transfer of existing assets in exchange for money. The compensation paid to labor as a proportion of the sales price in a static transaction is often very little.

The installation (labor) of a used part (a static asset) produces a transaction that may be equal parts dynamic and static. But calculating the dynamic component of individual transactions is less important than understanding the impact of public policies that favor employment-minimizing transactions.*

The Financial Sector
Compared with companies in the real economy, firms in the financial

---

* This emphasis on the labor content of a transaction highlights the importance of employment in a modern economy. This is similar to the way that utility theory distinguishes between levels of satisfaction in economic activity that are not reflected by monetary value alone. Unlike a thousand-dollar dynamic transaction, a billion-dollar static transaction that puts nobody to work may do nothing to benefit human survival.

sector can handle very large dollar volumes of transactions with very few people. A big manufacturer may need ten thousand employees to earn $5 billion in gross revenue. A large financial firm engaged in some combination of investment banking, insurance, commercial lending, or brokerage work may handle $100 billion in transactions and earn $5 billion in revenue with only one thousand employees. Workers in the financial sector can earn higher compensation than people in the real economy. But a dynamic transaction in the real economy will typically put many more people to work than a transaction of similar size in the financial sector.

Financial firms provide services, and, as stated before, all services are dynamic transactions. But these financial services are often used to facilitate other transactions (e.g., real estate loans, brokerage activity, insurance, or more exotic activity like options or derivatives) that may be either static or dynamic.

A loan is a dynamic transaction (a service). It may fund a transaction such as the purchase of an existing building (static) or the construction of a new building (dynamic). These transactions are in the real economy and thus external to the financial sector. But peculiar to the financial sector, a dynamic transaction may have no impact at all on the real economy.

Suppose a financial firm designs a derivative product that will effectively insure a company against an unfortunate event; e.g., a dramatic increase in the price of some raw material. The company uses funds in a financial sector account to pay the derivative seller, who deposits the money in the financial sector. In the unlikely event that the company collects on the derivative, it will deposit the funds it receives in the financial sector.

Note that this transaction resides entirely in the financial sector. It benefits neither the company's customers nor its suppliers. It consists entirely of financial services and has no impact on the real economy. We call this an *internal dynamic financial transaction.*

This example helps explain how massive amounts of money can be made using financial instruments like derivatives, futures, and options, in transactions that have no impact, static or dynamic, on the real economy. No one is suggesting that this activity is illegal, only that it consists almost entirely of the movement of money and paper with little labor component (i.e., there are few workers involved). No tangible goods are created. No nonfinancial services are rendered. It is just part of a large financial board game using real money and typically funded by participants in the real economy.

Another danger of internal dynamic financial transactions was brought to light in 1998 when Long Term Capital Management, an obscure Greenwich, Connecticut, investment fund, went under. LTCM couldn't meet its obligations on massive numbers of highly leveraged transactions worth billions. This threatened to produce a ripple effect of defaults and bankruptcies across global financial markets until investment bankers and the government stepped in to solve the problem.[79]

Chapter 15 addresses how excess wealth has to find a place to go and sometimes ends up in places like LTCM. Our concern here is that even under the best of circumstances, large amounts of money can be accommodated in the financial sector, one way or the other, without giving rise to many jobs.

Government, Taxes, and Employment

What is the overall impact of government on employment in the economy? The immediate effect of taxation is to divert money away from personal consumption and private sector investment. But government provides services, and services are dynamic transactions. Government services include planning and letting contracts for the construction of public goods, such as roads, bridges, and schools. These are built by private sector contractors, and their work is a dynamic process. Either government or private sector companies may be used to maintain these public properties, but in either case, the services provided are dynamic.

Often, big marketplace inadequacies in a big economy require big government remedies that employ large numbers of both white- and blue-collar workers. These jobs are especially critical in our technology- and capital-intensive modern economy, in which the private sector routinely minimizes the use of labor whenever possible.

People don't want to pay for government because that requires tax payments. (Wouldn't it be nice if everything were free?) But when we compare the impact on employment from public sector spending with that of both parts of the private sector (the real economy and the financial sector), the results are startling. Private sector economic activity includes massive numbers of expensive static transactions that, by definition, require little labor. As noted, the financial sector often facilitates static transactions and handles huge dollar volumes of financial services with very little labor (per transaction dollar). It can also tie up massive amounts of money in internal dynamic financial transactions with little labor and no direct impact on the real economy whatsoever.

Public sector spending, by contrast, consists almost entirely of dynamic activities. There is virtually no static component. Government provides necessities that can come from nowhere else while employing both public and private sector labor in jobs that would not otherwise exist.

It is easy to see how efforts to defy reality in a modern economy by arbitrarily reducing government have greatly diminished employment opportunities. This "lost" employment includes many clerical and construction jobs that don't require highly specialized skills. Per dollar spent, public sector transactions funded by tax revenue typically put more people to work than private sector transactions. The former are almost entirely dynamic; the latter have high static and financial sector components that minimize the use of labor.

We should resist arguments that private sector activity is better because it produces a higher multiplier effect in the economy than public sector spending. These multiplier effects are calculated using the dollar value of transactions. This obscures two important facts. First, private sector activity includes a high proportion of expensive employment-minimizing transactions. By contrast, government spending is made up almost entirely of dynamic transactions. Multipliers hide the remarkable job-creating ability of public sector spending.

Also, multiplier effects hide the fact that average compensation in public sector employment is reasonable but not spectacular. This includes many government contractor jobs. By contrast, private sector compensation can be much higher. But then it tends to create and aggravate maldistribution problems. That is the subject of chapter 15.

Economic Optimization

Well-known economic statistics can conceal defects in the economy that may even be life-threatening. Gross domestic product (GDP) says little about neglected infrastructure and the delays and frustrations that arise when driving on poorly maintained roads. There is no line item in GDP for people who forgo medical care because they lack health insurance. A low unemployment rate may obscure a high proportion of inadequate employment or hide a low labor force participation rate.

Public policy decisions require a broader view of economic activity than that described by many well-known economic measurements. We need to know the impact of taxation and government spending on consumption, employment, and business opportunities. How does public policy affect investment? Does it simply make more money available for investment while diminishing economic activity (demand) that motivates business expansion? We know that excessive accumulations of money (*surplus money*) in the financial sector tend to find their way to employment-minimizing "investments" like internal dynamic financial transactions. How can we create the best mix of private sector and public sector economic activity?

The country can achieve economic optimization when government provides necessities that can only come from the public sector. By performing its proper role in the economy, government creates jobs in both the public and private sector that would not otherwise exist. Since public sector transactions are almost entirely dynamic, economic optimization changes the mix of transactions to favor those that enhance employment.

The first step in economic optimization is to ensure the provision of the five categories of government described in chapter 1. The first four (total market irrelevancy, internal market defects, predominant market insufficiency, and acute market insufficiency) provide necessities that won't come adequately from anywhere else. Enough said about that. The fifth category, general market insufficiency, provides services that may pay off handsomely. They often lead to new products that spur economic activity and employment in the private sector.

The public sector provision of the five categories leads almost entirely to dynamic transactions (e.g., defense, road construction, education, health care, and funding basic research). By definition, these offer a high number of jobs per dollar (or per millions of dollars) of spending. These are typically middle-income jobs that meet the definition of adequate employment. If we measure economic activity in jobs and not in monetary value of transactions, the country typically gets more "bang for the buck" in public sector spending than in equivalent private sector spending.

The necessities provided by government can be paid for with taxes on the private sector, money that would otherwise be used for transactions that tend to reduce employment. Taxes on financial transactions, great inheritances, and high incomes are especially useful. They can help the country increase the dynamic (high employment) component of transactions in the economy. Tax policy should be designed to favor the high utility (i.e., high satisfaction) provision of necessities over mere increases in existing wealth. Taxation will be discussed further in chapter 15, where we address income and wealth distribution.

These policies not only increase fairness and political stability; they create a better economy for productive people at all income levels. Economic optimization would increase employment and personal consumption, reduce social services for the newly employed, provide more opportunities for private sector profits and investment, widen the tax base, increase growth, and favor the productive rich over the unproductive rich, all while fulfilling unmet needs.

Economic optimization uses the inescapable fact that in a modern economy $E = M + G$ to achieve an optimal allocation of resources to their best alternative uses. This optimal allocation can only occur if government and taxation are used to compensate for market deficiencies. These deficiencies include pure market forces that would offer extra mink coats and diamond rings to unproductive people while denying food and medical care to young children.

Public Sector Transactions

Economic optimization also requires adjusting public sector functions to accommodate changing circumstances. Consider a few of the issues that arise when the American people determine necessary government transactions:

- Politically motivated opposition to government has both reduced essential public services and artificially injected private sector firms into inherently public sector activities (e.g., Medicare Advantage plans). Common sense, pragmatism, and compassion should determine public policy. Contracting food services near, but not in, a war zone could be more efficient than expanding the military. But making every highway, street, and alley into a toll road in order to avoid raising taxes places an undue burden on lower-income people.

- Nationwide, publicly funded charter schools have had mixed results. Some have outperformed public schools while others have proven to be only entrepreneurial ventures that pursue profits while neglecting education. We must learn from the best and shut down the rest.

- Medicare Advantage programs created for ideological reasons have restricted choices of medical providers while subjecting patients to insurance companies with a financial incentive to deny coverage. But this experiment has been useful in one regard. It has reminded us that private sector, for-profit insurance companies are unnecessary. These companies were adequate when medicine had little to offer, but the usefulness of private sector insurers has been eclipsed by widespread and dramatic advances in medical care. The United States should use Medicare to insure everybody. Optimal fees and fair reimbursements to medical providers should be a matter of public policy. Private sector Medicare contractors could still be useful for purely administrative functions.

- In our complex modern economy, we should expect to occasionally encounter the need for additional government services. A looming example is the shortage of new antibiotics and other treatments for drug-resistant bacteria. These treatments are very expensive to develop and quickly become obsolete as bacteria evolve to thwart them. When these antibiotics work properly, they save lives. But by design, the treatment period is short. Compared with the sale of medications for chronic conditions, these drugs don't offer pharmaceutical manufacturers much opportunity for profit. Funding research and the development of new treatments for drug-resistant bacteria are classic Category I functions of government. The actual manufacturing would be done by private sector contractors.

- America needs to acknowledge that Social Security is the nation's retirement account. Labor market forces (unemployment and inadequate employment) prevent most people from adequately saving for retirement. Taxes on both carbon fuels and carbon emissions can provide some of the extra revenue needed to fully fund Social Security and other necessities like Medicare, infrastructure, and education. This tax may be regressive, but the programs it funds would be redistributive. People who pay disproportionately would benefit disproportionately.

- As a reminder, government services make up for inadequacies in the private sector and are provided as a matter of public policy after study and deliberation by the elected representatives of the people. The ongoing controversy over the National Flood Insurance Program is a reminder of both the nature of government services and why $E = M + G$. Opponents of the flood insurance program point out that it does not collect sufficient premiums to cover claims. This sounds suspiciously like the US Defense Department, the FBI, the US Supreme Court, the Coast Guard, and every other proper function of government, almost none of which can make money. If a public sector program could make money or break even without help from taxpayers, it might properly be viewed as a private sector market function. The National Flood Insurance Program exists and loses money precisely because, as a matter of public policy, Americans want to preserve the affordability of living in parts of the country subject to flooding.

- The United States Postal Service (USPS) is a constant source of irritation to antigovernment politicians who oppose the use of government for anything other than national defense and police protection. Like just about every other department in the federal government, the USPS loses money. But it is the only entity in the country that physically connects all the people to each other. Significantly, private for-profit delivery services like UPS and FedEx are among the USPS's biggest customers. It is just not economically feasible for them to deliver every-where. They will not make a two-hundred-mile round trip across Montana to earn a small delivery fee; so they ship the package via the USPS. Such built-in inefficien-cies account for much of the USPS's losses. At one time, the USPS was a Category I government function. Now we classify the USPS as Category V—it provides services that, in the judgment of the American people, the private sector alone cannot provide adequately.

Public sector services represent neither a preference for socialism nor a desire for big government. They are inherent features of a modern economy, and we resist them at our peril. As a critical part of the process of economic optimization, these government functions can ensure that the glass of economic prosperity doesn't have to be half-empty; the glass can be quite full.

Other than to acknowledge its importance, we have spent little time on private sector market activity. Our focus has been entirely on less appreciated aspects of modern economics: government, employment, and the nature of transactions. The next chapter covers another important topic, the distribution of income and wealth, where we once again face the imbalance between investment opportunities and the amount of money available for investment.

Chapter 15
Income and Wealth Distribution

The wealthy are an endless source of fascination to the multi-tudes who are one job loss, one major illness, or one more car or education loan away from financial distress. It's exciting to witness conspicuous consumption, even if only from the respectful distance afforded by television. Spending money is good, right? It enables businesses to profit, creates employment opportunities, and motivates investments and entrepreneurial activity.

Given half a chance, anyone is capable of throwing money around. But the wealthy are actually defined by their relative lack of consumption; that is, by the proportion of their after-tax income that they don't spend. Fifty people with an after-tax income of $20,000 each will together spend a million dollars annually simply to survive. One person with an after-tax income of $1 million could easily save or invest (i.e., not spend) $600,000 or more.

Nonconsumption

As we've seen, different types of consumption have a very different impact on employment. Big dynamic transactions, like buying newly built homes, will put a lot of people to work. But big static transactions just swap money for existing assets.

Even for the ultra-hedonistic, opportunities for dynamic personal consumption hit an upper limit. One can consume only so much food and drink, and partying is limited by the need for sleep. People who "shop till they drop" long enough will eventually drop.

In the 1970s, the wife of one Fortune 500 chief executive became famous for flying her friends halfway across the country in a private jet to have a fresh seafood lunch. This slovenly consumption at least had the virtue of being dynamic. By the time her husband put an end to it, she had become a living argument for a steeply progressive personal income tax.

By default, the wealthy will direct large sums of their extra money to employment-minimizing purchases of static assets like large estates, ranches, famous paintings, vintage autos, and expensive antiques. These huge static transactions may be as much investments as consumption. Even more of their money will go to the financial sector to buy existing shares of stock or for internal dynamic financial transactions, sometimes via hedge funds.

To be sure, millions of Americans have some financial assets in their IRA or 401(k) accounts. They may even own a little land, perhaps as a result of an inheritance. But we are concerned about the impact of huge accumulations of wealth held by only a handful of people. To what extent does this money stifle employment? Could a surplus of money available for investment actually do harm? Does great inheritance create a welfare state for the rich?

In nineteenth-century America, most people had little or no money. So rich families were the only source of funds for capital-intensive projects like railroad construction. But now we have a highly developed financial system in which the money in everyone's savings, checking, IRA, and 401(k) accounts is available for investment by Wall Street or by commercial banks acting as financial intermediaries.

Unfortunately, recent decades have witnessed an ever-increasing maldistribution of both income and wealth. Most people in developed countries suffered during the stagflation of the 1970s and early 1980s. But wealthy people could profit by

temporarily shifting discretionary funds to shares of oil companies and other entities that benefited from OPEC's control of the
oil markets. After market forces corrected stagflation (chapter
6), another economic force magnified the uneven distribution
of income and wealth: tax cuts became all the rage. In America's
progressive income tax system, tax cuts disproportionately benefited the wealthy while underfunding government spending that
worked to everyone's advantage.

Piketty's Work: Shining a Light on Maldistribution

Recently published research has shed considerable light on the
extent and significance of maldistribution in the world. Unfortunately, that light reveals nothing favorable to the vast majority of
Americans.

In 2014, French economist Thomas Piketty's *Capital in the
Twenty-First Century* summarized almost all that is known about
the distribution of income and wealth in the world. Research
by Piketty and other social scientists incorporated all reliable
data from all countries of the world. They often used ratios, say
of wealth to national income, to compare pure numbers (i.e.,
numbers devoid of units) and thus eliminate concerns about
inflation or currency exchange rates. This allowed comparisons
both over time and between countries. We will describe some of
the highlights of this very important and readily accessible book.

For most of human history, capital was composed almost
entirely of real estate such as land and buildings. By the twenty-
first century, however, capital in developed countries consisted
mainly of industrial and financial assets. Growth in the economy
is the sum of population growth and per-capita output growth.
Piketty noted that "When the rate of return on capital significantly exceeds the growth rate of the economy . . . , then it logi-

cally follows that inherited wealth grows faster than output and income." This condition, symbolized as $r > g$, has applied throughout most of modern history and is projected to apply in the remainder of the twenty-first century.[80]

Wealth can grow at a faster rate than the economy no matter who owns the wealth. Indeed, the wealth need not be owned by anyone. College endowment funds, for example, can grow faster than the economy. Anyone who inherits a large (and already invested) fortune will routinely get the advantage of this growth opportunity despite either their lack of merit or personal exertion. The central thesis of Piketty's book is that "an apparently small gap between the return on capital and the rate of growth can in the long run have powerful and destabilizing effects on the structure and dynamics of social inequality."[81]

Piketty notes that in "all known societies, at all times, the least wealthy half of the population own virtually nothing (generally little more than 5 percent of total wealth)"; the top 10 percent own between 60 percent and 90 percent of total wealth, and the remaining 40 percent (the middle class) own the remaining 5 to 35 percent.[82] Clearly, the survival of the great majority of the population is dependent on employment of some sort, not on returns from their investments.

Prior to World War I, this lopsided distribution of wealth in Europe may have actually been a good thing. The wealthy could partake of fine food, big houses, education, and opportunities to enjoy art, science, books, and travel. In a labor-intensive world, it took a great many servants, the downstairs help, to accommodate the upstairs lords and ladies. A more equal distribution of wealth would have relegated everyone to something between destitution and genteel poverty, and impeded the advancement of society on many fronts. "[W]ithout such inequality it would have been impossible for a very small elite to concern them-selves with something other than subsistence," says Piketty.[83] The wealthy took the benefits of inheritance and inequality as a given in society. Unlike today, "This view of inequality deserves credit for not describing itself as meritocratic, if nothing else."[84]

During and after the two world wars, a widespread apprecia-tion for the sacrifices that many people made produced a tempo-rary shift to a more egalitarian world. The wealthy paid higher taxes. Rich Europeans lost physical assets due to widespread destruction. In the United States, veterans were given educa-tional benefits (the GI Bill) and help with housing (VA loans). For a while, there seemed to be opportunities for all as countries recov-ered from the war and satisfied pent-up demand. It appeared that inheritance would be less important and that capital would be accumulated by effort and saving during one's own lifetime. Several generations, including America's baby boomers, grew up during this period. But the illusion of an egalitarian world would soon disappear.[85]

Since 1981, tax cuts and other domestic policies that favor the wealthy have returned some countries to pre–World War I distributions of income and wealth. The problem is particularly acute in English-speaking countries like the United States, which seem to have less concern about extreme differences in wealth. The upper 10 percent of the income hierarchy claimed 30 to 35 percent of US national income in the 1970s, but received 40 to 45 percent by the 2010s.[86] This can be attributed to the rise of "super managers" and to "positioning" (chapter 13), both of which allow compensation without rational upper limits.

By the early 2010s, income from labor in the United States was about as unequally distributed as has ever been observed anywhere.[87] During 2000–2010, income inequality in America had "regained the record levels observed in 1910–1920."[88] Income inequality and low inheritance taxes combine to produce extremes in wealth inequality. As we observed earlier, these large wealth accumulations typically grow faster than the rate of growth in the economy and do so without regard to merit or actual effort on the part of the owner.

Let's consider Piketty's analysis in light of what we have discussed in previous chapters. Our concerns about income and wealth distribution have nothing to do with envy. They are centered on the disconnection between people who live off the return of capital from huge accumulations of wealth, and the vast majority of the labor force who must work to support themselves in the modern economy. Unfortunately, the former may disassociate themselves from the general population. They may readily accept specious appeals to eliminate important government services that are essential to compensate for market inadequacies. Their disconnection from the concerns of the great majority can undermine democracy and reduce both employment opportunities and the availability of necessities. These problems are magnified if their great financial resources are allowed to affect the political process.

The maldistribution of income and wealth in Europe in the 1910–1920 period was fairly innocuous. In a labor-intensive world, there were millions of jobs for servants, field hands, and factory workers. This was a modern economy (i.e., no realistic possibility of self-sufficiency), but the list of necessities in life was still short—mainly food, clothing, and shelter—and reminiscent of a primitive economy.

In our technology- and capital-intensive world, employees are often just an inconvenient cost to be minimized. But Americans and most other people in the twenty-first century have one important thing in common with their nineteenth- and very early twentieth-century brethren. They live in a modern economy, an interconnected world where employment is critical for survival.

Piketty's concern about "destabilizing effects" on society suggest only that income maldistribution may combine with inheritance to allow 10 percent of the population to live very well on the return on capital of ever-expanding wealth that can be inherited in perpetuity. This could produce a welfare state for the rich while minimizing the already-meager per-capita assets of the masses. But this does not address another large concern: the increased proportion of employment-minimizing transactions caused by maldistribution.

Large family fortunes often hit upper limits on dynamic transactions for either personal consumption or good investment opportunities in the real economy. So, by default, accumulations of great wealth tilt the economy toward an excessive number of large static transactions and pure financial sector transactions, both of which tend to minimize employment.

Public policy that caters to this ever-increasing maldistribution of income and wealth represents an existential threat to the overwhelming majority of Americans, including most of the people who vote for these policies. We will offer some remedies shortly, but for now we only note that Piketty's concerns about instability are not misplaced. Americans will not always go to the slaughterhouse without protest.

In the current American political environment, antigovernment tactics require that, in anticipation of possible government remedies, some distractions (chapter 10) must be conjured up to obscure Piketty's warnings about maldistribution. These distractions are: Piketty is European, so brace yourself for "European socialism," whatever that is; and talk of maldistribution smacks of Communism.

In fact, the decades-long failure of Reaganomics has made Piketty's concerns much more applicable to the United States than they are to Europe.

Slicing the American Pie

Uneven distribution of income and wealth is a natural consequence of a market-dominated economy. But as we've seen, mere "uneven" distribution becomes maldistribution when its impact on the economy is decidedly negative. Let's take a closer look at the American version of the uneven distribution that, as Piketty states, appears in "all known societies, at all times."

One-half of the American population owns at most 5 percent of the nation's wealth. If we divide this 5 percent of the nation's wealth by about 160 million people, we see that their per capita wealth is nearly zero. In chapter 13, we noted that forces of supply and demand in the labor markets determine that throughout their lifetime, many people in the labor force are repeatedly subjected to inadequate employment, transitional unemployment, and intrinsic unemployment. It is not surprising that one-half of the population has accumulated virtually nothing. Their most valuable assets are their future claims to Social Security, Medicare, and other government services.

To understand wealth in the United States, we must look at the upper 50 percent of American wealth holders. The richest 10 percent of Americans have about 70 percent of the wealth, and the next 40 percent (the middle class) own about 30 percent. But Piketty warns us that the wealth of the upper 10 percent will tend to grow at a faster rate than the growth in the economy. So over time, even with an expanding economy, the 10 percent will increase their wealth at the expense of the middle class. The new wealth pie will eventually be divided into 75 percent and 25 percent slices, and well on the way to an 80 percent/20 percent split. Maldistribution will increase until good investment opportunities are diminished to the point that the return on capital is less than the growth rate in the economy. Good investment opportunities disappear when consumption (demand) is reduced as more and more workers are forced to accept inadequate employment.

There are numerous ways that this transfer of wealth from the middle class to the rich occurs. For example:

John fell on hard times. In order to at least temporarily maintain his middle-class status, John was forced to sell a parcel of land that he had inherited from his parents. The land was bought by a wealthy heiress who could afford to hold it for future appreciation.

Mary found herself in between jobs and had to use the money in her IRA to pay her bills. Now she has no retirement savings.

Bill lost his job and then his home in the Great Recession. His house was bought by a real estate holding company owned by a group of rich investors. Coincidentally, Bill now rents another home owned by that same company.

Since the 1980s, tax cuts have allowed wealthy people to amass more and more money. This money has to find a home, and that home might be yours. In 2015, a controversy erupted when lawmakers and community activists rallied in Washington to protest the sale of distressed mortgages by the federal government to private equity firms and hedge funds. The critics were concerned that these private buyers would be too quick to foreclose on the properties rather than allow borrowers to modify the terms of their loans.[89] Slowly but surely, assets are moved up the food chain to wealthier buyers and rich landlords.

The empirical evidence is not encouraging. The Federal Reserve System reports that at the end of 2013, median household net worth in the United States was only $81,200.[90] It is even more revealing to look at the Fed's net worth figures in 2013 dollars by age groups. The median net worth figures for the two age groups in their prime earnings years, those 40–49 years old and 50–59 years old, were only $68,000 and $137,000, respectively.[91] Social Security, a Category III function of government, will figure heavily in their retirement planning.

It is not just the lower 90 percent of the population that should be concerned by the prospect of having a smaller slice of America's net worth in the future. The richest 1 percent of the population will in time increase their fortunes at the expense of the next 9 percent. Economies of scale in portfolio management and opportunities for nontraditional investments allow larger fortunes to earn bigger returns than everyone below them in the economic food chain.[92] Increases in huge accumulations of wealth are inexorable, and these assets have to come from somewhere.

In January 2015, Oxfam International released a report indicating that the richest 1 percent of the world's population owned 48 percent of global wealth in 2014, up from 44 percent in 2009. By the end of 2016, the richest 1 percent will own more than half the world's wealth.[93] Anyone tempted to reject these statistics should remember that since everything from inheritance to political influence to tax policies to Thomas Piketty's r > g criteria favors the wealthy, it is quite plausible that, barring some remedy, the richest 1 percent could one day own 90 percent or more of the world's wealth.

Competition among the very wealthy will increase the value of high-dollar static assets such as fancy estates, vintage auto collections, and paintings by well-known artists. Even more surplus money will find its way into the financial sector. When good investment opportunities are exhausted, investors will resort to schemes using derivatives, exotic financial instruments, and toxic assets—the same types of assets that caused the Great Recession. Idle money is the devil's workshop.

Remedies to Wealth Maldistribution

Maldistribution of income and wealth is a naturally occurring problem in a market economy. It is not due to some market imperfection.[94] Just like other market problems, such as unemployment, inadequate employment, and employment minimizing transactions, maldistribution is a market inadequacy. Recall that the need for both Category III (predominant market insufficiency) and Category IV (acute market insufficiency) functions of government is determined by inadequacies in the private sector marketplace.

When government is used on a large enough scale to address the effects of market inadequacies (this is the proper economic role of government in a modern economy), it may diminish other problems. Additional public sector spending for necessities like infrastructure, defense, Medicaid, Social Security, and education will simultaneously increase the number of adequate jobs and reduce unemployment. In chapter 14, we called this process "economic optimization."

Changes in the tax system that fund economic optimization can also introduce taxes that minimize the damage to the economy caused by maldistribution. But higher marginal tax rates on the rich, an end to capital gains benefits, taxes on financial transactions, and taxes on carbon fuels and carbon emissions will not sufficiently diminish excessive wealth accumulation.

Since the 1980s, tax cuts that disproportionately benefit the rich have effectively been funded with borrowed money.

As a result, taxes that diminish maldistribution of wealth have often been recommended as a means to reduce the national debt. Thomas Piketty suggested a one-time tax on capital assets to raise money for debt repayment.[95] But there are other, more politically feasible ways to minimize the eternal problem of wealth maldistribution.

Estate and inheritance taxes offer the best opportunity to reduce maldistribution. The former taxes the dead; the latter taxes people who get something for nothing. Beyond some exempt amount (say, $6 million a year per person from all sources of inheritance), inherited money should be taxed at ordinary personal income tax rates. Existing gift (or transfer) taxes would still be necessary to keep people from thwarting the intent of estate taxes. Even when combined with a recommended increase in marginal tax rates, heirs would be taxed at a lower tax rate than lottery winners.

There is no need to express sympathy for either the "losses" suffered by the dead or the reduced inheritance of those who insist that they need a five-hundred-yard head start to run a one-hundred-yard race. It is important to the nation to diminish the undue influence of inheritance. The growth, without regard to merit, of large accumulations of wealth gives "lasting, disproportionate importance to inequalities created in the past." When this process is left unchecked, Piketty warns, "the past tends to devour the future."[96]

So what do the very wealthy think about all this? It's difficult to scientifically sample the opinions of billionaires. Warren Buffett has said that people like himself are not taxed enough. Buffett understands that with economic optimization, the nation will thrive and so will his investments in restaurants, furniture stores, insurance companies, and railroads.

The concept of taxing wealth is not as outrageous as some people have been led to believe. In 1999, Donald Trump himself, then merely an outspoken Republican real estate magnate, proposed a onetime "net worth tax" of 14.25 percent on individuals and trust funds worth more than $10 million to pay off the national debt.[97] At a minimum, our modern technology- and capital-intensive economy requires a tax structure that simultaneously funds economic optimization and eliminates counterproductive wealth accumulation.

Anecdotally, it seems that wealthy people who are capable of making money (the productive rich) are amenable to higher taxes. Those who merely inherit wealth are reduced to demanding tax cuts. This partly determined our classification of the wealthy in chapter 13. The productive rich work and contribute to earnings from their capital investments. They are members of the labor force. The unproductive rich are classified as nonemployed. The former can profit from a higher tax but more dynamic economy; the latter cannot.

American economic history tells us that the productive rich are productive at every marginal rate of personal income taxation, ranging from 28 percent to 90 percent. They will not refuse the opportunity to make, say, an extra $1 million in pretax income just because taxes are high. This is true even though they don't actually need any more after-tax income for consumption. The rich operate at a zero-to-low level of marginal utility, i.e. the satisfaction (or utility) that they receive from incremental amounts of money is low. After all, their needs will have already been met by income taxed at lower rates. Any extra money they earn can always be put in the financial sector or spent on large static investments.

Note that increased tax rates require higher pretax earnings to net any given amount of money. These higher tax rates can actually be used to spur extra economic activity by wealthy yet acquisitive people who consume products at a low level of marginal utility. In other words, unduly low taxes on rich people may sap their motivation.

In America, it is possible for people to amass great wealth, sometimes at levels that border on the comical. Whether the money comes from earnings or inheritance, the wealthy benefit disproportionately from what the country has to offer. So they rightfully pay a disproportionate share of taxes.

The dynamic nature of public sector transactions (chapter 14) ensures that government revenue from high taxes on the wealthy contributes more to the economy than anything the wealthy are likely to do with additional after-tax money. But rich people have enough political clout to promote the misguided notion that low taxes on the wealthy are beneficial to the economy. The facts say otherwise. In the words of Nobel Prize–winning economist Paul Krugman: "Bill Clinton's tax increase was followed by a huge economic boom, the George W. Bush tax cuts by a weak recovery that ended in financial collapse. The tax increase of 2013 and the coming of Obamacare in 2014 were associated with the best job growth since the 1990s. Jerry Brown's tax-raising, environmentally conscious California is growing fast; Sam Brownback's tax- and spending-slashing Kansas isn't."[98]

Taxation on the unproductive rich should always be at marginal rates greater than or equal to the rates on the productive rich. Capital gains should never be taxed at a lower rate than income earned from productive labor. The risk of sitting around and doing nothing while waiting for a profit on the sale of a static asset is overrated.

Failure to Thrive

The best way to understand the benefits of what we termed economic optimization is to look at what happens when there is insufficient redistribution via taxation and government. So let's review some recent economic history.

Perhaps 95 percent of Americans were adversely affected by the stagflation of the 1970s and early 1980s. The other 5 percent were either people who profited directly from the temporary boom in the oil industry or who were among the wealthy Americans with discretionary money to invest in oil-related companies. The collapse in oil prices in the mid-1980s was widely beneficial (chapter 6). Almost everyone had extra money to spend. Rich people could shift their investments out of oil and into a wide variety of other opportunities. The country hadn't yet felt the full impact of decades of maldistribution from tax cuts.

Since the 1980s, decades of insufficiently progressive taxation have put more and more surplus money into the hands of wealthy Americans. But these same policies were detrimental to the overwhelming majority of Americans who benefit from the redistributive effects (including jobs) of government programs. This created an imbalance: too much money for investment and too little money in the hands of middle- and low-income Americans whose consumption creates investment opportunities.

This imbalance helps explain two recent phenomena. First, the shale-fracking boom from 2008 to 2014 received disproportionate attention from lenders and investors because the oil industry was about the only thing that seemed to offer growth potential. There simply weren't enough investment opportunities to absorb all the money held by the wealthy.

Second, when greater oil production began to flood the market in 2014, the nation didn't benefit as much from lower energy costs as it did in the mid-1980s. Most Americans weren't going anywhere economically, and lower gasoline prices didn't help all that much. They used the extra money in their pockets to pay down debt. Rich people could disinvest in the oil industry but didn't have many other good options in which to park their extra money.

The failures of Reaganomics at the state level (chapter 9) provide other examples of why rejecting government's critical place in the economy creates an economic implosion. We saw how resistance to government and insufficient taxation in Kansas, Louisiana, and Texas diminished the provision of education, health care, and public sector jobs, and caused both budget reductions and neglect of the poor. At every level of government, it seems that public policy designed to benefit the wealthy creates an unhealthy economy.

Even with declining unemployment, the economy is sluggish. Most Americans don't have much money to spend. A political environment that favors the rich sees wages as a cost of business, not as a driving force for consumption and investment. This stifles economic activity. A healthy economy tends to produce at least slightly higher prices as people compete for output and resources. But for years, inflation has actually been too low for the Federal Reserve Bank to justify increasing its key interest rate much above zero.

America lacks sufficient redistribution. The country needs more public sector spending that reduces the costs of higher education, vocational training, and health care; creates jobs by funding more infrastructure maintenance and construction; increases most people's Social Security payments; expands pre-K education; and provides more social services. This is not a "stimulus plan"; it simply describes the proper role of government in a modern economy. Redistribution via economic optimization would expand opportunities for business investment by increasing employment and consumption.

Capitalist countries with policies that we would label economic optimization include some of the happiest, healthiest, and most prosperous nations on earth. So why do Americans resist the redistributive requirements of a modern economy? The United States has a much more diverse population than happy countries like Sweden and Denmark. It is easy for some American politicians to tell their constituents that when they pay taxes to fund economic optimization, it only benefits those "other" people, the ones who are not like them. In fact, it benefits everybody.

Americans must be on guard against anything that keeps the system from working properly. At various times, these threats may include too little government, inadequate tax revenue, insufficient government regulation, excessive government regulation, maldistribution of income and wealth, government inefficiency, private sector government contractor inefficiency, those who do not fully understand government's role in the economy, and politically motivated attacks designed to sabotage the system. The five categories of government functions described in chapter 1 rank with life, liberty, and the pursuit of happiness, among the things that really matter in America.

Chapter 16
Public Policy

The modern economy is a combination of private sector markets and government. Markets satisfy demand for most, but not all, necessary goods and services. But markets have problems, which we labeled irrelevancy, insufficiency, and internal defects. These problems led to the five categories of government functions that are so important for a properly functioning economy.

To satisfy our needs, we shop at markets and we vote for government. Stated another way, we vote for markets by spending money there and we shop government by making good policy decisions. The use of the public sector to meet important needs is not some twentieth-century political creation; history tells us that economists have long recognized a necessary role for government.

Economic History

Economists long ago resolved the controversy over whether or not market problems are self-correcting. Jean-Baptiste Say (1767–1832) offered the Law of Markets, the classical notion that the market's output automatically injected just the right amount of payments to the factors of production (land, labor, and capital) to purchase the output produced. But Say's Law was undermined both by savings and by purchases of imported goods. As a result, markets could suffer from overproduction due to lack of demand. There is simply no reason to believe that market problems are automatically self-correcting. At times, nonmarket solutions are the only option.

In the Great Depression (chapter 3), Republican president Herbert Hoover was forced to use the federal government for job creation, although he did so mainly by offering big infrastructure contracts to private companies. Democrat Franklin Roosevelt dramatically expanded the use of government to include direct federal government hiring, among many other things. Desperate times often call for realistic measures.

The use of government to stimulate demand in a slumping economy is attributed to the great neoclassical economist John Maynard Keynes (1883–1946). Since the successful application of Keynesian economics in the 1930s and 1940s, Keynes has been the favorite target of anyone trying to use natural antigovernment bias for political advantage. But of all the great economists, Keynes and British merchant banker (investment banker) David Ricardo (1772–1823) were the two most successful participants in the market economy.

Keynes managed an investment trust, served as an officer of an insurance company, ran a working farm, made money in international markets (art, currency, books) and in stocks, and financed theatrical productions, all while earning a good living as a writer, academic, and government official. In the years after World War I, he made "a fortune worth then two million dollars."[99]

Keynes's work in economics was designed to preserve the free-enterprise system that had profited him so handsomely. But he knew that sometimes government functions were necessary to compensate for market inadequacies. The fact that some politicians have had success in using Keynes as a symbol of government overreach speaks more to the gullibility of the audience than to any defect in Keynes.

Markets always work in the sense that, under all conditions (peace or war, good weather or bad, too little or too much regulation, high or low unemployment, etc.), markets move toward an equilibrium of supply and demand. But government must be an essential part of the economy if all needs are to be met. Free-market purists say otherwise, but a modern economy with no public services invites disaster. People would not be able to get to work or to the market to buy necessities; the country would descend into illiteracy, third-world status, and chaos; and the nation would eventually be taken over by more advanced countries that saw the value of government for many things, including a conquering army.

But for generations, it has been easy to combine natural anti-government bias (chapter 2) with America's historic opposition to government (chapters 3–5) to gain political advantage. People were so confused about the market correction to the stagflation of the 1970s and 1980s (chapter 6), that it was possible to proclaim that antigovernment policies had solved the problem. This confusion has continued (chapters 7–9), encouraged by distractions and deceptions (chapter 10) that have created the political problems Americans must deal with every day (chapters 11–12).

It is hardly a radical notion to suggest that an economy requires both private sector markets and public sector government, at least according to Adam Smith (1723–1790), an icon for advocates of free-market capitalism. In his masterwork, *An Inquiry into the Nature and Causes of the Wealth of Nations* (1776), Smith lists three duties of government that he deems to be "of great importance." They are (1) national defense, (2) "protecting, as far as possible, every member of society from the injustice and oppression of every other member of it, or the duty of establishing an exact administration of justice," and (3) "erecting and maintaining certain public works and certain public institutions" that private sector individuals could not profitably erect and maintain.[100]

Adam Smith's eighteenth-century insight that government has important roles to play in an economy is extraordinary. He would surely have approved of the expansion in public education required by advances in technology, the sciences, and the social sciences. Private sector individuals cannot profitably erect and maintain institutions for universal public education.

Smith would have understood the importance of civil rights laws, the police, and regulation of business, to protect ourselves "from the injustice and oppression of every other member" of society.

Recent experiences have verified the need for government, something that was so obvious to Adam Smith. Inadequate financial regulation to protect us from the "injustice and oppression" by others has given us both the S&L crisis and the LBO fiasco in the 1980s, and more recently, the Great Recession. Neglect of government's role in "erecting and maintaining certain public works" has led to crumbling and inadequate infrastructure. It is unfortunate that people are so easily attracted to appealing but unworkable economic theories that ignore Smith's pragmatic views.

Failed Theories

Karl Marx (1818–1883) was understandably concerned about the plight of workers in the Industrial Revolution. The modern economy at the time had not yet incorporated proper functions of government to mitigate the "injustice and oppression" that Adam Smith warned about. Society lacked child labor restrictions, minimum wage requirements, regulations promoting workplace safety, and laws mandating health insurance and workmen's compensation. Marx saw the evils of industrial capitalism, but he didn't live long enough to see the benefits that mass production and entrepreneurialism would bring to ordinary people.

Applications of Marxist theory failed because they excessively favored a public sector "command economy" over private sector markets. While there were several proximate causes of the demise of the Soviet Union (chapter 8), it could never keep up with the West economically. Successful modern economies must include proper doses of both markets and government. An imbalance invites unnecessary suffering, even disaster. The Communists insisted on too much government; capitalists typically advocate too little government.

In the United States, the Cold War–era view of a pure market economy is very much alive, largely because it is simplistic enough to be politically useful. But the success of Keynesian economics and the obvious need for many of the government programs introduced by the New Deal and the Great Society have caused Americans to think more deeply about the nature of their economy. Such thinking, however, was a clear threat to the closely held beliefs of antigovernment factions that had originally coalesced around Republican presidential candidate Barry Goldwater in 1964 (chapter 4). They needed a theory to counteract Keynesian economics. This begat supply-side economics.

Supply-side economics is designed to turn attention away from government and back to the private sector. It suggests that supply will increase, prices will be lower, and unemployment will decrease if we cater to "producers" by favoring them with lower marginal tax rates and less regulation. But problems with this theory arise immediately. The proper economic functions of government described in chapter 1 exist precisely because markets alone are inadequate to meet the needs of the people. None of these inadequacies are addressed by supply-side economics. The need for regulation, for example, doesn't go away just because miscreants in the business sector are left unregulated.

While reducing taxation on low- and middle-income people

will certainly increase consumption, it may jeopardize funding for government services that greatly benefit these same people. As for those with higher incomes, history has shown us that productive high-income people are still productive at marginal income tax rates as high as 90 percent. Moreover, sufficiently high taxes on wealthy people and their heirs are essential to mitigate the employment-minimizing effects caused by maldistribution of income and wealth (chapters 14 and 15).

We now know (chapters 7–9) that Reaganomics, the nation's grand experiment with supply-side economic theory, has been a disaster. Markets alone eliminated America's economic problems in the 1980s while Reaganomics has a 100 percent failure rate. This latter fact is a predictable consequence of the requirements of our modern economy. Ironically, Reaganomics is only useful as a guide for what *not* to do in economic policy.

There never was a time in US history that general opposition to the American government made any sense. We look to government when there are problems with markets, the weather, acts of war, or terrorism. When there are problems with government itself, then the solutions invariably come from government (elections, investigations, congressional hearings and debates, court cases, and changes in the law).

But the collapse of the Soviet Union in the early 1990s was widely interpreted in the West as a victory of markets over government. This, along with years of confusion about the "success" of Reaganomics, invited further applications of antigovernment policy, all doomed to failure. Since 2007, the United States has been rewarded with the Great Recession, a huge increase in the national debt, and a dysfunctional Congress, none of which had to happen.

Equilibrium in a Modern Economy

Markets work to provide us with goods and services for which there is demand (i.e., both willingness and ability to buy) sufficient to allow profitable sales. We may even proclaim that markets always work toward an equilibrium of supply and demand. Hungry people without money will be deprived of food in order to achieve equilibrium: zero supply equals zero effective demand. Nonprofit organizations may or may not alleviate their hunger. Only a systematic solution—e.g., government-provided food stamps—can be relied on to solve their problem.

Clearly, the equilibrium we seek is a broader concept than mere "market equilibrium." Market theory does not readily accommodate the presence of people in society, a huge complication. Perhaps the worst form of market inadequacy is the failure to incorporate the fact that human life is important.

Equilibrium in a modern economy occurs when the availability of necessities equals the need for necessities. By now it should be clear that efforts to achieve this equilibrium must include the five categories of government functions; it is foolish to expect markets alone to satisfy all our needs. Indeed, Americans must be wary of market problems that tend to prevent this equilibrium.

Maldistribution of income and wealth leads to large numbers of employment-minimizing transactions (chapters 14 and 15). At the same time, constant efforts to minimize labor costs combine with other market forces to create unemployment and inadequate employment, both of which deprive people of resources that are essential for survival. It is easy to understand how market forces naturally lead to less than optimal levels of employment and aggregate demand. Also, the combined effect of maldistribution and insufficient aggregate demand yields an excess of money available for investment while at the same time reducing opportunities for useful investments.

Unfortunately, a modern economy naturally tends toward increasing maldistribution. Piketty's $r > g$ criteria (chapter 15) is inexorable. Left unchecked, maldistribution may reduce many people to selling valuable assets more often than they buy them. In the wake of the Great Recession, one of the hottest businesses in the country was the purchase of gold and silver from Americans trying to pay their bills. So a properly designed public policy must minimize the impact of maldistribution of income and wealth.

Pervasive inadequacies in private sector markets provide us with an opportunity to replace market activities that cause problems with public policies that solve problems. The concept of economic optimization described in chapter 14 will create a healthier economy (less unemployment, increased consumption, more output, more investment opportunities, greater growth). Necessary government services can be paid for with a tax structure that can be adjusted to minimize excessive wealth accumulation.

We can summarize all of this by listing the characteristics, including essential government functions, of a modern economy in equilibrium:

- Markets provide goods and services at will.
- The public sector becomes the source of those necessities that markets are not fully capable of providing for some reason. These are the first four categories of government functions described in chapter 1.
- Public sector spending increases the proportion of dynamic transactions (i.e., labor-intensive transactions) in the economy. The increased employment leads to more consumption, business profits, and investment, while reducing the need for some Category IV functions

of government. This increased employment converts some people from recipients of government aid to taxpayers.

- The public opts for Category V government functions for many reasons, including increased business activity and job creation.

- Public sector spending and proper tax policies favor dynamic transactions while minimizing maldistribution of income and wealth. Key features of this tax system include sufficiently progressive marginal rates on high income; an end to any capital gains tax advantages; taxes on both carbon fuel and carbon emissions, with revenue allocated to infrastructure, education, Medicare, Social Security, and alternative energy sources; adequate estate and transfer taxes; a tax at ordinary rates on inheritance above an annual threshold; and a financial transactions tax. The carbon fuel and emissions taxes are the only burdensome taxes on this list. They will likely raise prices for any product made using carbon fuels (oil, natural gas, coal). But these admittedly regressive taxes will be paid disproportionately by those who benefit disproportionately from the programs that they fund.

Because of misguided resistance to government's proper role in a modern economy, the United States has never reaped the rewards of the economic structure (markets, public sector spending, taxation) described earlier. Economic optimization creates growth. It replaces employment-minimizing transactions with dynamic transactions in the form of government spending on necessities that will not come from private sector markets.

Public Sector Necessities

At no time in American history has there ever been a movement for "big government" just for the sake of "big government." The first four functions of government described in chapter 1 provide necessities that, for one reason or another, will not come from markets. People have used their opposition to these public sector functions to get elected to office, but the need for these necessities never goes away.

Some government functions are so obviously essential that even antigovernment politicians reluctantly support them. National defense (Category I), Social Security (III), veterans' health care (III), and law enforcement (I) come to mind. But market inadequacies determine the need for all of the categories of government described in chapter 1.

There is considerable opposition to adding public services that are clearly necessary in a modern economy. But universal pre-K education and greatly reduced costs for postsecondary education and training (III) simply recognize that a K–12 education alone is inadequate in our modern technology- and capital-intensive economy. Universal health care (IV) is an obvious necessity. Adequate business regulation (II) will help us avoid past mistakes like the Great Recession that caused unnecessary suffering for millions of Americans.

As a reminder, the modern economy ("E") is made up of essential contributions from both markets ("M") and government ("G"), symbolically $E = M + G$. Unfettered by economic reality, markets will degenerate into ever-increasing maldistribution of income and wealth, low labor force participation, pervasive inadequate employment, an excess of investment funding over investment opportunities, and an overemphasis on financial speculation (internal dynamic financial transactions).

Communism failed as an alternative to a market economy

because it did not strike the proper balance between markets, government, and democracy. Capitalism must avoid the same mistakes. It is essential for the public sector to perform its proper roles in our modern economy if the great majority of Americans are to survive and prosper. That is the public sector imperative.

Future Economic Research

Perhaps one day, for the first time in history, Americans will consciously use public policy to fulfill the requirements of a modern economy. There are several opportunities for economists to do useful research to facilitate the adjustment toward this economic reality and away from the current system (overemphasis on market mythology, neglect of government, and confusion about economic history).

The list of necessities in a primitive economy (food, clothing, shelter, some degree of security) was short compared to that in our capital- and technology-intensive modern economy. People working in a complex, interconnected system also require education and training (for themselves and their children), transportation (a car or access to public transportation), communication (usually a phone of some sort), medical care (it's hard to work if you're sick or dying), retirement savings (people want to live even when they are too old to work), and several forms of security (police, homeland security, and national defense).

The poverty level ($23,850 a year for a family of four in 2015) greatly understates the costs of all these necessities. The level of income and benefits necessary to avoid inadequate employment is a far more accurate measure of what it takes to survive in a modern economy. On a before-tax basis, it may be twice the poverty level. This figure will vary with both family size and geographic differences in the cost of living. We need annual calculations of the compensation needed to achieve adequate employment both with and without government benefits. This would provide a measure of how much individual assistance hardworking people need to compensate for market inadequacies.

Recall that government spending is "dynamic," a technical term that reflects the relatively large number of jobs created per dollar spent in the public sector compared with alternative uses of money in the private sector for static or financial sector transactions. Government jobs per tax dollar spent can be measured. It is more difficult, however, to measure employment per dollar spent in the financial sector, where massive numbers of transactions typically require little labor input. Derivative transactions of various kinds (forwards, futures, options, swaps, collateralized debt obligations) are especially opaque.

Static transactions occur in both the real economy and the financial sector. The dollar value of static exchanges, if publicly available, may yield numbers that are staggering. We are particularly interested in the dollar amounts of large static transactions (both for consumption and investment) by wealthy and high-income people.

We also need measurements that reveal employment as a function of transaction type. In particular, what is the impact on employment of, say, a billion dollars of tax revenue from high- income taxpayers that is spent on public sector necessities (Categories I–IV)? This could be contrasted with the impact on employment of a billion dollars in discretionary funds retained (i.e., not paid in taxes) by high-income taxpayers.

We can measure the added employment from incremental public sector spending. Can we also measure (1) any resulting reduction in unemployment, (2) the proportion of new jobs that meet the local requirements of adequate employment, (3) the reduction in welfare spending due to newly hired workers, (4) the proportion of new government jobs versus new private sector (i.e., contractor) jobs, and (5) the multiplier effect of this additional economic activity?

Because of the multiplier effect, the numerical reduction in unemployment in the economy can exceed the increased number of workers directly involved in incremental public sector spending. Note that if personal income tax rates are sufficiently progressive, then the likely alternative private sector uses of the tax revenue that funds this public sector spending would have created less employment. Why? At the margin, spending by high-income taxpayers tends toward static transactions and internal dynamic financial transactions, neither of which produce many jobs per dollar spent.

In our modern technology- and capital-intensive economy, people are subjected to both market deficiencies and market efficiencies. The former give rise to the five categories of government functions in chapter 1. But there is widespread opposition to the use of government for anything. When we minimize public sector functions and also minimize the cost of labor in the name of efficiency, this leads to reductions in employment, consumption, aggregate demand, business activity, and investment opportunities. At what point do we render the economy unworkable for a large part of the population? Are we there yet? Currently, low unemployment statistics do not translate into economic prosperity for most working Americans, mainly due to inadequate employment. Can we determine the combination of private sector efficiency, government minimization, and maldistribution that leads to revolution?

Much of the benefit of economic optimization comes from providing ourselves with public sector goods and services that are not available from markets. Dollars alone do not capture the full value of national defense, Social Security, infrastructure, public education, and Medicare.

We should add universal, single-payer health care; universal pre-K education; and low-cost post-secondary education and training. These essential public services offer employment that would not otherwise exist, jobs that help offset the private sector's continuous efforts to minimize employment costs. Is it possible to construct a cost/benefit analysis of these incremental government services that fully incorporates their contribution to better health, increased job opportunities, and reduced welfare costs?

Government is critically necessary to compensate for both deficiencies and efficiencies in our modern, market-dominated economy.

Acknowledgments

I would like to thank my younger daughter, Kathryn McGuire, for her assistance in the preparation of the manuscript. Without her encouragement, this book would not have been possible.

Notes

Chapter 1

1   David McCullough, *John Adams* (New York: Simon & Schuster, 2001), 433.

Chapter 3

2   "Herbert Hoover," Newworldencyclopedia.org, accessed January 7, 2014, http://www.newworldencyclopedia.org/entry/Herbert_Hoover.

3   John D. Hicks, George E. Mowry, and Robert E. Burke, *The American Nation* (Boston: Houghton Mifflin Company, 1963), 543–45.

4   John Maynard Keynes, *The General Theory of Employment, Interest, and Money* (New York: Harcourt, 1964), originally published on February 3, 1936.

5   "United States Presidential Election, 1960," Wikipedia, accessed September 17, 2015, https://en.wikipedia.org/wiki/United_States_presidential_election_1960.

Chapter 4

6   *No Fear: U.S. Constitution & Other Important American Documents* (New York: Sparks Publishing, 2006), 22–23.

7   Ibid. 52.

8   Samuel Eliot Morison and Henry Steele Commager, *The Growth of the American Nation* (New York: Oxford University Press, 1962), 349–50.

9   Michael P. Malone and Richard W. Etulain, *The American West: A Twentieth-Century History* (Lincoln, Nebraska: University of Nebraska Press, 1989), 220–32.

10   Mark Potok, "Intelligence Report: Land Use & the 'Patriots,'" The Southern Poverty Law Center, Fall 2014, 27.

11   Ibid. 30.

12   Morison and Commager, *The Growth of the American Nation*, Appendix.

13   Potok, "Land Use & the 'Patriots,'" 27.

14   Harold Maass, "Sandra Day O'Connor's Second Thoughts on the 2000 *Bush v. Gore* Decision," Yahoo News, April 30, 2013.

15   Lottie L. Joiner, "Remembering Civil Rights Heroine Fannie Lou Hamer: 'I'm Sick and Tired of Being Sick and Tired,'" The Daily Beast, September 2, 2014, http://www.thedailybeast.com/articles/2014/09/02 remembering-civil-rights-heroine-fannie-lou-hamer-i-m-sick-and-tired-of-being-sick-and-tired.html.

16   Robert Dallek, "Presidency: How Do Historians Evaluate the Administration of Lyndon Johnson?" History News Network, George Mason University, September 18, 2015.

17   *1964*, PBS documentary, viewed March 18, 2014.

Chapter 5

18   Robert A. Caro, *The Years of Lyndon Johnson: The Passage of Power* (New York: Alfred A. Knopf, 2012), 223–24.

19   Thomas E. Ricks, *Fiasco: The American Military Adventure in Iraq* (New York: Penguin, 2006), 193, 250–56.

20   Daniel Yergin, *The Prize: The Epic Quest for Oil, Money, and Power* (New York: Simon & Schuster, 1991), 625.

21   Ibid. 634.

22   "Historic Inflation United States-CPI Inflation," accessed February 6, 2015, www.inflation.eu/inflation-rates/united-states/historic-inflation/cpi-inflation-united-states.aspx.

23   William Greider, *Secrets of the Temple: How the Federal Reserve Runs the Country* (New York: Touchstone, 1987), 149.

24   Ibid. 188.

Chapter 6

25   Amoco Production Company, New Orleans Regional Office, Geophysical Department, 1973–1980.

26   Yergin, *The Prize*, 27.

27   Ibid. 666.

28   Thomas Piketty, *Capital in the Twenty-First Century* (Cambridge: The Belknap Press of Harvard University, 2014), 445.

29   Yergin, *The Prize*, 654.

30   Ibid. 660–61.

31   Ibid. 665–750.

32   "Consumer Price Index, All Urban Consumers-(CPI.U), U.S. city average, All items, 1982–84=100," US Department of Labor: Bureau of Labor Statistics website, last accessed August 15, 2012, http://www.bls.gov.

33   "Gross Domestic Product," July 27, 2012, Bureau of Economic Analysis website, last accessed August 16, 2012, , http://www.bea.gov/national/xls/gdpchg.xls.

34   "The National Unemployment Rate," Bureau of Labor Statistics website, last accessed August 15, 2012, http://www.bls.gov.

35   "Bond Yields and Interest Rates: 1900–2002-Con.," US Census Bureau website (Statistical Abstract of the United States), http://www.census.gov/statab/hist/HS-39.pdf, 2003.

Chapter 7

36   Greider, *Secrets of the Temple*, 412.

37   Timothy Curry and Lynn Shibut, "The Cost of the Savings and Loan Crisis: Truth and Consequences," FDIC Banker's Review website, last accessed June 25, 2013, https://www.fdic.gov/bank/analytical/banking/2000dec/brv13n2_2.pdf.

38   Steve Fraser, *Wall Street: A Cultural History* (London: Faber and Faber, 2005), 495.

39   T. Boone Pickens, *Boone* (Boston: Houghton Mifflin, 1987), 149–260.

40   "US Government Defense Spending History and Charts," www.usgovernmentdefensespending.com briefing, last accessed September 28, 2015.

41   Ibid.

42   Jonathan Weisman, "Reagan Politics Gave Green Light to Red Ink," *Washington Post*, June 9, 2004, http://www.washingtonpost.com/wp-dyn/articles/A26402-2004Jun8.html.

43   Ibid.

Chapter 8

44   Lou Cannon and *TIME* contributors, *The Reagan Paradox: The Conservative Icon and Today's GOP* (New York: TIME Books, 2014), 22.

45   NBC video, nbclearn.com website, last accessed May 30, 2015, https://nbclearn.com/portal/site/K-12/flatreview?cuecard=33292.

46   Owen Ullman, *Stockman: The Man, the Myth, the Future* (New York: Donald I. Fine, 1986), 174.

47   Ibid. 167.

48   Ibid. 241–243.

49   Associated Press, "Bush Honored with 'Courage Award' for Unpopular Tax Hikes as President," *Houston Chronicle*, May 5, 2014.

Chapter 9

50   Bill White, *America's Fiscal Constitution: Its Triumph and Collapse* (New York: Public Affairs, 2014), 3.

51   Joseph E. Stiglitz, *Freefall: America, Free Markets, and the Sinking of the World Economy* (New York: W. W. Norton & Company, 2010), 18–19.

52   Tim Jones (Bloomberg News), "Tax Cuts Force Kansas Schools to Close Early," *Houston Chronicle*, May 6, 2015.

53   Max Ehrenfreund, "Kansas Tax Cuts for Rich Create Budget Shortfalls," *Houston Chronicle*, April 22, 2015.

54   Tim Jones, "Brownback to Cut Pensions, Roads to Close Kansas Budget Deficit," Bloomberg Business, December 10, 2014, http://www.bloomberg.com/news/articles/2014-12-10/brownback-to-cut pensions-roads-to-close-kansas-budget-deficit.

55   Margaret Newkirk(Bloomberg News), "'Duck Dynasty' Keeps Tax Break as Jindal Cuts Louisiana Colleges," *Houston Chronicle*, May 6, 2015.

56   Alia Wong, "Bobby Jindal, Budget Cuts, and the Uncertain Fate of Louisiana's Universities," *The Atlantic*, May 7, 2015, www.theatlantic.com/education/archives/2015/05/bobby-jindal-budget-cuts-and-the-uncertain-fate-of-louisiana's-publicuniversities/392552/.

57   Piketty, *Capital in the Twenty-First Century*, 538.

Chapter 10

58   "The CRA and Subprime Lending: Discerning the Difference," Banking and Community Perspectives, Federal Reserve Bank of Dallas website, last accessed June 26, 2013, http://www.dallasfed.org/assets/documents/cd/bcp/2009/bcp0901.pdf.

59   Suzi Parker, "Big Bird Will Haunt Mitt Romney," *Washington Post*, October 4, 2012, http://www.washingtonpost.com/blogs/she-the-people/wp/2012/10/04/big-bird-will-haunt-mitt-romney/.

60   Robert Parry, "Time for PBS to Go?" reclaimthemedia.org, last accessed March 26, 2014, http://www.reclaimthemedia.org/media_literacy_bias/time_for_pbs_to_go%3D5152.

61   Cannon and *TIME* contributors, *The Reagan Paradox*, 153.

62   Mike Ward, "Abbott Order Makes Waves," *Houston Chronicle*, April 3, 2015.

63   Joe Keohane, "How Facts Backfire," *Boston Globe*, July 11, 2010, www.boston.com/bostonglobe/ideas/articles/2010/07/11/how_facts_backfire/.

64   https://www.youtube.com/watch?v=6BEsZMvrg-I, last accessed September 18, 2015.

65   Leonardo Maugeri, "The Virgin Oil Fields of Iraq," *Newsweek*, July 5, 2004.

66   Matthew Simmons, *Twilight in the Desert: The Coming Saudi Oil Shock and the World Economy* (New York: John Wiley & Sons, 2005).

67   David Corn, "WATCH: Rand Paul Says Dick Cheney Pushed for the Iraq War So Halliburton Would Profit," Motherjones.com, April 7, 2014, www.motherjones.com/politics/2014/04/rand-paul-dick-cheney-exploited-911-iraq-halliburton.

Chapter 11

68   Michael Scherer, "Up With People," *TIME*, July 20, 2015.

69   Belinda Luscombe, "10 Questions," *TIME*, May 21, 2012.

70   Don Lee, "Poverty Rate and Incomes Stay Stagnant," *Houston Chronicle*, September 17, 2015.

71   Ibid.

Chapter 12

72   Josh Israel, "Bob Dole Scolds GOP: Reagan Wouldn't Make It in Today's Republican Party," Thinkprogress.org, May 26, 2013, http://thinkprogress.org/politics/2013/05/26/2062861/bob-dole-scolds-gop/?mobile=nc.

73   Cannon and *TIME* contributors, *The Reagan Paradox*, 118.

74   Ibid. 83.

75   Ibid. 83.

76   J. M. Roberts, *History of the World* (New York: Oxford University Press, 1993), 903.

Chapter 13

77   Piketty, *Capital in the Twenty-First Century*, 332–35.

78   Christopher Rugaber, "Why U.S. Job Openings Are Surging, While Hiring Is Lagging," *Houston Chronicle*, September 10, 2015.

Chapter 14

79   Roger Lowenstein, *When Genius Failed* (New York: Random House, 2000). (Provides an excellent account of LTCM's rise and fall.)

Chapter 15

80   Piketty, *Capital in the Twenty-First Century*, 26.

81   Ibid. 77.

82   Ibid. 336–37.

83   Ibid. 415.

84   Ibid. 416.

85   Ibid. 381.

86   Ibid. 294.

87   Ibid. 256.

88   Ibid. 321.

89   Mathew Goldstein, "Senator Joins Protest of Sale of Mortgages," *Houston Chronicle*, October 1, 2015.

90   "Americans' Net Worth Rises to Record High," *Houston Chronicle*, September 19, 2014.

91   Scott Burns, "Big Dogs Running Faster than the Rest of the Pack in Net Worth," *Houston Chronicle*, May 25, 2015.

92   Piketty, *Capital in the Twenty-First Century*, 450.

93   Associated Press, "Richest 1 Percent May Soon Own Half of Wealth," *Houston Chronicle*, January 20, 2015.

94   Piketty, *Capital in the Twenty-First Century*, 573.

95   Ibid. 527.

96   Ibid. 378.

97   Michael Scherer, "The Donald Has Landed," *TIME*, August 31, 2015.

98   Paul Krugman, "Fantasies and Fictions at the GOP Debate," *Houston Chronicle*, September 19, 2015.

Chapter 16

99   Robert L. Heilbroner, *The Worldly Philosophers* (New York: Simon & Schuster, 1972), 252.

100   Adam Smith, *An Inquiry into the Nature and Causes of the Wealth of Nations* (Indianapolis: Liberty Press/Liberty Classics, 1981), 687–688. This reference is from the chapter on Adam Smith in Charles Sackrey, Geoffrey Schneider, and Janet Knoedler's *Introduction to Political Economy* (Boston: Dollars & Sense, 2010), 36–39.

Bibliography

Cannon, Lou and *TIME* contributors. *The Reagan Paradox: The Conservative Icon and Today's GOP*. (New York: TIME Books, 2014).

Caro, Robert A. *The Years of Lyndon Johnson: The Path to Power*. (New York: Alfred A. Knopf, 1982).

_____*The Years of Lyndon Johnson: Means of Ascent*. (New York: Alfred A. Knopf, 1990).

_____*The Years of Lyndon Johnson: Master of the Senate*. (New York: Alfred A. Knopf, 2002).

_____*The Years of Lyndon Johnson: The Passage of Power*. (New York: Alfred A. Knopf, 2012).

Fraser, Steve. *Wall Street: A Cultural History*. (London: Faber and Faber, 2005).

Gilbert, Michael Douglas. *America in the Economic World: Jobs, Necessities, and Economic Optimization*. (Minneapolis: Langdon Street Press, 2014).

Greider, William. *Secrets of the Temple: How the Federal Reserve Runs the Country*. (New York: Touchstone, 1987).

Heilbroner, Robert L. *The Worldly Philosophers*. (New York: Simon & Schuster, 1972).

Hicks, John D., George E. Mowry, and Robert E. Burke. *The American Nation*. (Boston: Houghton Mifflin Company, 1963).

Isaacson, Walter. *Einstein: His Life and Universe*. (New York: Simon & Schuster, 2007).

Keynes, John Maynard. *The General Theory of Employment, Interest, and Money*. (New York: Harcourt, 1964).

Lowenstein, Roger. *When Genius Failed*. (New York: Random House, 2000).

Malone, Michael P., and Richard W. Etulain. *The American West: A Twentieth-Century History*. (Lincoln, Nebraska: University of Nebraska Press, 1989).

McCullough, David. *John Adams*. (New York: Simon & Schuster, 2001).

Morison, Samuel Eliot, and Henry Steele Commager. *The Growth of the American Nation*. (New York: Oxford University Press, 1962).

Pickens, T. Boone. *Boone*. (Boston: Houghton Mifflin, 1987).

Piketty, Thomas. *Capital in the Twenty-First Century*. (Cambridge: The Belknap Press of Harvard University, 2014).

Ricks, Thomas E. *Fiasco: The American Military Adventure in Iraq*. (New York: Penguin, 2006).

Roberts, J. M. *History of the World*. (New York: Oxford University Press, 1993).

Sackrey, Charles, Geoffrey Schneider, and Janet Knoedler. *Introduction to Political Economy*. (Boston: Dollars & Sense, 2010).

Smith, Adam. *An Inquiry into the Nature and Causes of the Wealth of Nations*. (Indianapolis: Liberty Press/Liberty Classics, 1981).

Stiglitz, Joseph E. *Freefall: America, Free Markets, and the Sinking of the World Economy*. (New York: W. W. Norton & Company, 2010).

Ullman, Owen. *Stockman: The Man, the Myth, the Future*. (New York: Donald I. Fine, 1986).

White, Bill. *America's Fiscal Constitution: Its Triumph and Collapse.* (New York: Public Affairs, 2014).

Yergin, Daniel. *The Prize: The Epic Quest for Oil, Money, and Power.* (New York: Simon & Schuster, 1991).

Index

About the Author

Michael Gilbert's primary interests in economics are in the related areas of survival in a complex modern economy, and in the proper relationship of government to private sector activity. He is the author of *America in the Economic World: Jobs, Necessities, and Economic Optimization* (Langdon Street Press, 2014).

Michael has graduate degrees in mathematics and business administration. He has been an exploration geophysicist since 1974. Michael's background in economics and geophysics uniquely qualifies him to analyze the market correction to stagflation in the 1980s and the widespread confusion that followed the improvements in the American economy.